casual aga cooking

sarah whitaker

with photographs by
simon burgess

Food preparation:
Sarah Whitaker
Food styling:
Sarah, Clementine and Daisy Whitaker and **Simon Burgess**
*(all the photographs are of the actual recipes and
once we had finished, we ate the lot!)*
Photographs:
Simon Burgess

There is probably no such thing as an original recipe. If I have inadvertently duplicated anyone else's ideas, I apologise – sometimes I think there must be a spy in my kitchen when I see a television cook make a dish that I invented the day before!

Details of demonstrations, further copies of this book
and copies of Sarah's other recipe collections:
Home Made in Nether Wallop
Relaxed Aga Cooking
and
The Twelve Days of Aga Christmas
are available from:
The Trout, Nether Wallop, Hampshire, SO20 8EW
e mail: kitchen@sarahwhitaker.com
www.sarahwhitaker.com
www.theagalady.com

casual
aga
cooking

sarah whitaker
with photographs by
simon burgess

for Anthony, with love
and
for Daisy, Clementine and James, uncomplaining guinea pigs!

'Aga' and 'Rayburn' are registered trademarks of Aga Foodservice Group plc

'Bake-O-Glide'™ is a reusable non-stick, coated cooking material manufactured by Falcon Products Ltd and available from cookshops and from Aga shops

First published in Great Britain in 2009 by
Sarah Whitaker
The Trout, Nether Wallop, Stockbridge, Hampshire, SO20 8EW
www.sarahwhitaker.com
www.theagalady.com

ISBN 978-0-9554306-2-6

Produced by The Choir Press, Gloucester
Printed in Great Britain

contents

getting to know your aga or range cooker

It is perfectly possible to cook on an Aga for 30 years and never use any of the cast iron cooking techniques. Lots of people do. They may wonder why the cooker loses heat, but love the cooker so much that they don't mind, much. Then they learn a few simple techniques, keep the lids down and cook more in the ovens and – as if by magic – the cooker stops losing heat and they never look back. If this is you, read on . . .

Life with an Aga is like a friendship. Its warm, benign presence in the kitchen is such a comfort in the house. It will cook any food you want, quickly or slowly, perfectly. From a slow-roasted Christmas turkey to a piece of toast, it is the ultimate cooker. For some people, it is the cast iron monster in the kitchen, frightening in the extreme – all those doors and no visible controls, where on earth do you start?

Put simply, an Aga has two hot plates: the left hand *boiling plate*, is very hot – it boils. The right hand, *simmering plate*, is about half the temperature of the boiling plate – it simmers. The two-oven Aga has a top, *roasting oven*, which is very hot – it roasts, and a lower, *simmering oven* that is about half the temperature of the roasting oven – it simmers. The three-oven Aga has an additional *baking oven* that runs at a perfect temperature for baking, about half way between the roasting and simmering ovens. The four-oven Aga also has a *warming oven*, cooler than the simmering oven. And that's it.

The Aga is a heat storage cooker; it maintains heat until the lids are opened for too long or cool food is put into the ovens, when the thermostat kicks in and the heat gradually regenerates. 80% of all cooking on an Aga takes place in the ovens, saving heat and fuel. This has the added benefit of no spitting fat to clear up and no cooking smells – the ovens are vented to the flue and all smells just disappear up the chimney.

You should never need to turn it up or down – don't go near that dial, except to vacuum away the dog hairs occasionally! Please don't turn the Aga up if you are cooking for a party – you will only burn things, as it will be much hotter than you are used to! It may cook a little more slowly if the ovens are very full, but it will be consistent and reliable.

Many of these recipes refer to hanging the tins and shelves from the runners at the sides of the ovens. Always count the runners downwards from the top of the oven. Hanging roasting and baking tins from the runners uses less space – you can fit much more into the ovens at once!

a note about ingredients

I have deliberately not specified organic, free range or unrefined ingredients in my recipes. The choice is up to you, the cook.

I prefer to use good quality, seasonal, locally produced fresh ingredients, rather than those imported from around the world, out of season and context. I am not convinced that all imported 'organic' foods meet the strict UK standards. For example, I use local bacon in preference to imported pancetta, as I can see pigs in the fields nearby.

I will not use any ingredient that I cannot easily buy locally – it seems so unfair to say that a recipe will only work if you use particular herbs gathered by fairies in the Provençal moonlight or a certain brand of olive oil only available from one Italian delicatessen in a back street in Islington or through the internet!

That said, I am very fortunate to live on the Hampshire/Wiltshire border, where wonderful farmers' markets, fresh fish and traditional butchers are found in abundance.

preparing ahead

In many of these recipes I have said that the food can be prepared ahead – to be cooked and either kept warm, or cooled and reheated to eat later or the next day.

Many of these dishes freeze really well, either part-cooked, or ready to defrost and serve. I tend to wrap dishes for freezing in kitchen paper, which absorbs any liquid given off during defrosting, to save things from becoming watery.

This does not mean that you *have* to make things in advance, just that you can, if it suits you to do so.

pea and ham roulade

To feed more people: Make two roulades for a starter for 16 or more. Try rolling the roulade along its long side for a longer, thinner roll to cut into more slices!

Serves 6–8 as a starter,
4 as a main course

10 oz (275g) frozen peas

½ tsp sugar

Salt and pepper

4 eggs

Filling:

Sprig of fresh mint

Tub (300g) cream cheese

½ tsp sugar

Salt and pepper

Pack (150g) Black Forest ham

Oven:

Baking oven, 180C, 250F, Gas 4

Prepare in advance:

Cooked, cooled and filled roulade

will keep in the fridge for 24 hours

Freeze:

No, the peas give off a lot of water

as the roulade defrosts

1 Put the peas into a pan and cover with water. Bring to the boil on the boiling plate, then drain at once. Plunge the hot peas into a bowl of very cold water, then drain and plunge them into another bowl of fresh very cold water. This is to cool them quickly and set the bright green colour.

2 Drain the now-cold peas and tip into a processor. Season with the salt, pepper and sugar. Whizz.

3 Separate the eggs and add the yolks to the processor and whizz to a bright green sludge.

4 Whisk the egg whites, then fold in the pea purée.

5 Line a large roasting tin with Bake-O-Glide and spread the pea mixture over it and bake

6 *3 and 4 oven Aga*: Hang the tin from the 3rd runners in the baking oven and bake for about 11 minutes until puffed up and beginning to brown.

7 *2 oven Aga*: Hang the tin from the 4th runners in the roasting oven with the plain shelf on the 2nd runners. Bake for about 9 minutes until puffed up and beginning to brown.

8 Take the cooked roulade from the oven and turn it out onto a clean, dry tea towel. Remove the Bake-O-Glide and roll the roulade up, starting with its short side, in the towel and leave to cool.

9 Set the cream cheese onto the back of the Aga to soften while the roulade cools.

10 Mix the soft cream cheese with the seasonings and chop in the mint. Unroll the cooled roulade and spread with the cream cheese mixture. Lay the slices of ham over the cheese then re-roll the roulade. Wrap in the tea towel or cling film and chill for at least an hour so that the cream cheese sets and holds it all together.

11 Serve in slices, with a little salad on the side of the plate.

twice baked goats' cheese soufflés in tomato sauce

I know, this has become THE ubiquitous starter, but for a very good reason – it always works, freezes brilliantly and is quite impressive!

To feed more people: Double the ingredients will fill 14 or even 16 ramekins if you are not too generous. You will need three times the quantity of sauce for 16 ramekins.

Serves 6

For the soufflés:

½ pint (300ml) milk

2 cloves

½ small onion

1 bayleaf

2 oz (55g) butter

2 oz (55g) plain flour

Pinch mustard powder

5 oz (150g) firm goats' cheese

2 eggs

3 tbsp freshly grated Parmesan

Handful fresh basil leaves

2 tbsp olive oil

Salt and pepper

For the sauce:

1½ lb (750g) plum tomatoes

1 tsp caster sugar

2 oz (55g) butter

3 tbsp olive oil

1   Cut the onion into 3 pieces and put it into a pan, with the cloves, bayleaf and milk. Bring to simmering point then cover and set aside to marinate for a few minutes.

2   Melt the butter in a pan on the simmering plate and use some of it to brush 6 ramekin dishes. Put the prepared ramekins into the small roasting tin to keep them together as they cook.

3   Stir the flour into the remaining melted butter and blend together. Strain the milk, discarding the bits, and slowly add the milk to the flour and butter, stirring all the time.

4   Put the pan onto the simmering plate and gently bring to the boil, stirring all the time. Remove from the heat once it has bubbled for a minute.

5   Crumble the cheese and add it, with the mustard powder and seasoning, to the thick sauce and beat together.

6   Separate the eggs and beat the yolks into the sauce. Whisk the egg whites and fold them into the mixture.

7   Pile the mixture into the prepared ramekins and hang the tin from the 4th runners in the roasting oven for about 20 minutes until they are risen and golden. Take the soufflés from the oven and watch them sink as they cool.

8   When the soufflés are cool, run a round bladed knife around the inside of each ramekin and tip out the soufflé. Put into an ovenproof dish, browned top uppermost.

twice baked goats' cheese soufflés in tomato sauce *continued*

Oven:

Simmering oven, 130C, 250F, Gas 1 and roasting oven, 200C, 400F, Gas 6

Prepare in advance:

Prepare the soufflés and the sauce and refrigerate for up to 24 hours

Prepare ahead:

Will keep warm for up to 30 minutes in simmering oven

Freeze:

Yes, before second cooking time. Bake from frozen for 30 minutes

9   For the sauce: Cut the tomatoes in half and put them into a deep sauté pan with the butter. Heat for a few minutes on the simmering plate, then cover and transfer to the simmering oven for about half an hour, until they are soft. Tip into a processor or liquidizer and whizz, or pass through a sieve. Stir in the olive oil, sugar and seasoning. Return the sauce to the pan and put it, uncovered, onto the floor of the roasting oven for 15 minutes to reduce and thicken.

10 To finish and cook the soufflés, pour the sauce around the soufflés in the ovenproof dish, tear up the basil leaves and scatter them over the top, with the grated Parmesan.

11 Set the grid shelf on the 4th runners and put the dish onto it and bake for about 20 minutes until the soufflés have magically risen and puffed up again!

cheese biscuits
for drinks

Makes about 25

5 oz (150g) plain flour

4 oz (110g) butter

3 oz (85g) grated Parmesan cheese

1 tsp cayenne pepper

Up to 5 tbsp water

2 tbsp sesame seeds

2 tbsp poppy seeds

Oven:

Baking oven, 190C, 375F, Gas 5

Prepare in advance:

Biscuit mix will keep in the fridge for up to 48 hours

Prepare ahead:

Biscuits will keep in an airtight tin for 48 hours (if you hide it)

Freeze:

Uncooked biscuit mix, slice and bake from frozen

1 Measure the flour, butter, cheese and cayenne into a processor and whizz until the consistency of breadcrumbs.

2 Add the water, a little at a time, until the mixture comes together as a stiff dough.

3 Divide the dough in half and roll one half into a long sausage then roll in the sesame seeds. Roll the other half into a sausage shape and roll in the poppy seeds.

4 Wrap each roll of biscuit mix in cling film and chill or freeze until firm.

5 Slice the rolls into ½"/¼ cm slices and lay into a baking tray lined with Bake-O-Glide and bake.

6 *3 and 4 oven Aga*: Slide the tin onto the 2nd runners in the baking oven and bake for about 12 minutes until golden brown.

7 *2 oven Aga*: Put the grid shelf onto the floor of the roasting oven and set the tin onto it. Slide the plain shelf onto the 3rd runners and bake the biscuits for about 8–12 minutes until golden brown.

8 Take the biscuits from the oven and let them stand for a couple of minutes to firm up before transferring to a cooling rack.

smoked cod balls
with pea sauce

To feed more people: Double the ingredients will make up to 10 portions, carefully divided between the plates. Double the sauce and three times the fish will serve up to 15. To make extra fish balls, just make them smaller!

Serves 4

For the balls:

8 oz (225g) smoked cod loin (it comes boneless and skinless)

4 oz (110g) cheddar cheese

3 egg whites

2 tbsp crème fraîche

Pinch of ground mace

Salt and pepper

For the sauce:

8 oz (225g) frozen peas

3 egg yolks

¼ pint (150 ml) single cream

¼ pint (150 ml) natural yogurt

Salt and pepper

To finish:

1 oz (25g) red Leicester cheese

Oven:

Simmering plate

Prepare ahead:

Cooked cooled balls and sauce will keep, separately, in the fridge for 24 hours

Prepare in advance:

Will keep warm in simmering oven for up to half an hour

Freeze:

Uncooked fish balls will freeze

1 Grate the cheddar – in a processor is fastest.

2 Change the processor blade and tip in the rest of the fish ball ingredients and whizz to a paste. Chill until needed.

3 For the sauce: put the peas into a pan, cover with water and bring to the boil. When boiling, drain and tip into a processor and whizz, with the rest of the sauce ingredients.

4 Tip the sauce back into the warm pan and set on the simmering plate and heat slowly, stirring all the time, until the sauce has thickened a little. Do not let it boil or you will have green scrambled eggs! Cover the sauce and set on the side of the Aga while you cook the fish balls.

5 Bring a large, fairly deep pan of water to the boil, then add the fish paste, a tablespoon at a time.

6 The balls will rise to the surface as they cook. Simmer them for about 4 minutes, then lift out of the water with a slotted spoon and drain on kitchen paper.

7 Pour the sauce onto individual plates, put the fish balls on top and then grate over the red Leicester cheese. As the plates come to the table, this will be melting onto the fish balls.

cheese and bacon potato pancakes

To feed more people: Double the mixture will make 16 small pancakes to divide among a group.

Serves 4

1½ lb (650g) floury potatoes

1 tbsp olive oil

3 oz (85g) smoked streaky bacon

½ medium onion

1 clove garlic

4 oz (110g) plain flour

1 egg yolk

4 oz (110g) Cheshire cheese

Oven:

Simmering oven, 130C, 250F,

Gas 1, simmering plate

Prepare in advance:

Cakes will keep in fridge for 24

hours before cooking

Prepare ahead:

Keep warm in simmering oven for

half an hour

Freeze:

Uncooked cakes

1 Cut the potatoes into even sized pieces and put into a pan. Cover with cold water and bring to the boil. When boiling hard, drain off all the water, cover tightly and put into the simmering oven for half an hour to cook.

2 Meanwhile, chop the onion finely and crush the garlic. Cut the bacon into small pieces. Heat the oil in a heavy based pan and add the onion, bacon and garlic. Transfer to the floor of the roasting oven for 5 minutes, shaking occasionally, until browned. Remove from the oven and allow to cool.

3 When the potatoes are soft, remove from the oven and mash until smooth. Mash in the flour, egg yolk and onion / bacon mixture. Crumble in the cheese and mix well. Leave to cool if time allows.

4 Form the mixture into 8 equal portions and shape into round patties – use flour on your hands to make it easier.

5 Lay a piece of Bake-O-Glide on the simmering plate and cook the potato cakes for about 4 minutes each side, until golden brown. Serve hot.

hummous

To feed more people: This quantity makes a lovely dip for up to 10, double the quantity should be enough for 25 to dip pitta bread or vegetables into with drinks.

1 tin (340g) chickpeas

2 tbsp tahini paste

1 clove garlic

½ tsp ground cumin

Juice of half a lemon

2 tbsp olive oil

Prepare ahead:

Keep in the fridge for up to a week

Freeze: No

1   Open the tin of chickpeas and drain the liquid away.

2   Put all the ingredients into a food processor and whizz until blended.

3   Serve with pitta bread, puffed up on the simmering plate.

aubergine dip for picnics

As a dip with drinks and other nibbles, this will go round 20 people.

Serves 6–8

1 large aubergine

1 tsp ground cumin

½ pint (200g pot) natural yogurt

Handful of chives

1 tbsp lemon juice

Salt and pepper

8 pitta breads

Oven:

Boiling plate

Prepare in advance:

Dip will keep in the fridge for up to 48 hours

Freeze:

No, the aubergines disintegrate as they defrost!

1   Put a griddle pan into the roasting oven (if it has a metal or removable handle) to heat up.

2   Cut the aubergine into ½" / 1cm slices.

3   Transfer the pan to the boiling plate and lay in the slices of aubergine – you may need to do this in two or three batches. Grill for about 4 minutes each side. Leave the grilled slices on a cooling rack to allow the steam to escape as they cool.

4   Pile the cooked aubergine into a processor; add the yogurt, cumin, lemon and seasoning. Snip the chives into the bowl then whizz briefly to chop the aubergine and mix everything together.

5   Turn into a bowl and serve with torn, toasted pitta breads to dip into it.

chicory, fig and roquefort bake

To feed more people: Double the ingredients will serve 10 as a starter – you will not need double the amount of olive oil!

Serves 4–6

1 lb (450g) chicory heads

8 fresh figs

8 oz (225g) Roquefort cheese

Salt and pepper

4 tbsp olive oil

Oven:

Roasting oven, 200, 400F, Gas 6

Prepare in advance:

Assemble the dish and refrigerate for 12 hours before baking

Prepare ahead:

Keep warm for 30 minutes in simmering oven

Freeze:

No, the chicory goes sludgy as it defrosts!

1. Trim the chicory heads and figs and cut into quarters lengthways. Put into a large bowl.

2. Cut the cheese into small cubes (or just crumble it in your fingers).

3. Add the olive oil and seasoning and gently mix everything together.

4. Tip into an ovenproof baking dish.

5. Set the grid shelf on the floor of the roasting oven and put the dish onto it. Bake for about 10 minutes until the chicory is browned and the cheese has melted.

6. Serve with bread to mop up the melted cheese and chicory juice.

warm mushroom pots

To feed more people: Double the ingredients will fill up to 10 ramekins

Serves 4 as a starter, 2 as a main course – can be served tepid or warm

12 oz (350g) chestnut mushrooms

1 onion

1 clove garlic

2 tbsp walnut oil

2 eggs

3 tbsp single cream or milk

1 tsp Dijon mustard

Salt and pepper

Sauce:

1 tin (340g) chopped tomatoes

1 tsp balsamic vinegar

Oven:

Baking oven, 160C, 350F, Gas 4

Prepare in advance:

Cooked, cooled pots will keep in the fridge for up to 24 hours. Chill sauce separately

Prepare ahead:

Keep warm beside the Aga for an hour

Freeze: *No*

1 Brush the inside of 4 ramekin dishes with oil.

2 Chop the mushrooms. Peel and chop the onion and crush the garlic.

3 Heat the remaining oil in a heavy based pan and add the mushrooms, onion and garlic. When sizzling, cover and put into the simmering oven for 10 minutes to soften.

4 While the mushrooms are in the oven, make the sauce: Tip the contents of the tin of tomatoes into a pan and add the balsamic vinegar. Season and set onto the simmering plate: bring to the boil then cover and transfer to the simmering oven for about 20 minutes.

5 Tip the cooked mushroom mixture into a processor and whizz. Add the eggs, milk and mustard and whizz until thoroughly mixed.

6 Pour the mushroom gloop into the ramekins, the put them into the small roasting tin and cover with foil.

7 *3 and 4 oven Aga*: Hang the tin from the 3rd runners in the baking oven and cook for 20 – 25 minutes until set.

8 *2 oven Aga*: Hang the tin from the 4th runners in the roasting oven and slide the cold shelf onto the 2nd runners. Bake for about 20 minutes until set.

9 Take the sauce from the simmering oven and purée it – either in a processor or with a hand blender.

10 To serve: put a puddle of sauce onto each of 4 plates, then turn out a mushroom pot onto it. Garnish with a little chopped parsley.

mushroom tarts tatin

To feed more people: Make the tarts in a 12-hole muffin tin – the tarts will be smaller (use a 3"/7.5 cms pastry cutter), but you should get 12 out of the pastry, using 12 slightly smaller mushrooms and double the quantity of pine nuts, olives and anchovies.

Serves 4

1 pack (375g) ready rolled puff pastry

4 large field mushrooms

1 tbsp olive oil

1 clove garlic

Sprig fresh lemon thyme

2 tbsp pine nuts

12 black olives

1 small tin anchovy fillets

Salt and pepper

Bag fresh salad leaves

2 tbsp French dressing

½ oz (15g) fresh Parmesan

Oven:

Roasting oven, 200C, 400F, Gas 6

Prepare in advance:

Cook and cool the mushrooms, assemble with the pastry in the tin and chill for up to 24 hours before cooking

Prepare ahead:

Will keep warm in the simmering oven for half an hour – do not turn out or the pastry will go soggy

Freeze:

No, the mushrooms get rubbery as they defrost

For a vegetarian version, use a green olive tapenade instead of the anchovies.

1 Wipe the mushrooms. Line the small shallow baking tray with Bake-O-Glide.

2 Chop the garlic and strip the leaves from the thyme. Drain the anchovies and roughly chop them. Crush the garlic.

3 Lay the mushrooms in the tray and dribble over the olive oil and thyme leaves. Season well.

4 Hang the tin from the lowest runners in the roasting oven and cook the mushrooms for about 15 minutes.

5 When the mushrooms are cooked, leave to cool for a while, then lift into the four holes of a 4"/10cms Yorkshire pudding tin. Scatter the pine nuts, anchovies, garlic and olives over the mushrooms.

6 Unroll the pastry and cut out four 6"/15cms rounds and lay a circle of pastry over each mushroom, pressing the edges down around the mushrooms.

7 Set the Yorkshire pudding tin in the grid shelf on the lowest runners in the roasting oven and bake for about 10 minutes until the pastry is puffed up and golden.

8 When cooked, invert the tin onto a square serving plate and lift off the tin. Grate a little fresh Parmesan cheese over the tatins.

9 Serve with a little salad tossed in French dressing.

coriander mushrooms

Serious mushrooms on toast!

To feed more people: Double the quantity will make 10 portions as a starter, but you wil need 5 ciabatta rolls.

Serves 4, can be served tepid or warm

1 lb (450g) chestnut mushrooms

1 lemon

1 tbsp coriander seeds

2 Thai lime leaves

3 tbsp olive oil

Salt and pepper

1 tbsp chopped fresh coriander

2 ciabatta rolls

Oven:

Simmering oven, 130C, 250F, Gas 1

Prepare in advance:

Keeps in the fridge for up to 2 days

Prepare ahead:

Keep warm beside the Aga for an hour

Freeze:

No, the mushrooms go slimy as they defrost

1 Cut the mushrooms into quarters.

2 Squeeze the juice of the lemon over the mushrooms.

3 Crush the coriander seeds and lime leaves.

4 Heat the oil in a heavy pan on the simmering plate and add the coriander seeds and lime leaves. Swirl over the heat until they start to pop, then add the mushrooms in the lemon juice and seasoning well.

5 When the mushrooms are sizzling, cover and transfer to the simmering oven for 10 minutes to soften.

6 Put the ciabatta rolls into the roasting oven for 3 minutes to warm up, then split them and put one half roll onto each of 4 plates.

7 Serve the mushrooms on the rolls, scattered with chopped fresh coriander.

serious beans on toast

To feed more people: Double the ingredients will make 10 starter-sized portions

Serves 4

1 tbsp olive oil

1 onion

1 clove garlic

1 tbsp sun dried tomato purée

1 tin (400g) chopped tomatoes

Sprig fresh thyme

Salt and pepper

Pinch sugar

4 oz (110g) smoked bacon

1 tin (400g) mixed beans

1 small ciabatta loaf

2 oz (55g) butter

Oven:

Simmering oven, 130C, 250F, Gas 1

Prepare in advance:

Beans taste even better after 24 hours in the fridge!

Prepare ahead:

Keep warm for up to half an hour, but do not set the beans onto the toast until just before eating

Freeze:

Cooked beans, yes

1 Peel and chop the onion, crush the garlic. Drain the tin of beans.

2 Heat the oil and add the onions and garlic. When sizzling, cover and transfer to the simmering oven for 10 minutes to soften.

3 Add the tomatoes and tomato purée to the cooked onions, add the herbs, sugar and seasoning, stir and bring to the boil. When boiling, cover again and return to the simmering oven for a further 10 minutes.

4 When the tomato mixture is cooked, add the beans. Set the pan on the simmering plate to boil.

5 Chop the bacon and put into a heavy based pan on the floor of the roasting oven for 5–7 minutes to brown and crispen. Tip the cooked bacon into the bean pan and stir together.

6 Slice the bread and toast it – on the simmering plate gives more control over the colour of the toast!

7 Spread the butter over the slices of toast, put onto plates and spoon the beans over before serving.

cauliflower, leek and ham soup

To feed more people: Double the quantity will fill 10 starter-sized soup bowls.

Serves 4–6

1 medium cauliflower

3 leeks

1 medium potato

4 oz (110g) piece ham or gammon

1 oz (25g) butter

1 medium onion

2 cloves garlic

1 tbsp olive oil

1½ pints (800ml) stock

4 tbsp cream

Chopped parsley to garnish

Oven:

Simmering oven, 130C, 250F, Gas 1

Prepare in advance:

Will keep in the fridge for up to 48 hours

Prepare ahead:

Keep warm in the simmering oven for an hour

Freeze:

Yes, before adding cream

1. Peel and finely chop the onion and garlic. Cut the cauliflower into florets and trim and slice the leeks. Cut the potato and ham into small cubes.

2. Melt the butter and oil together in a heavy based pan and add the onion and garlic. Stir over the heat until sizzling. Cover and put into the simmering oven for 15 minutes to soften. Add the cauliflower, leek, potato and ham to the cooked onions. Stir in the stock, bring to the boil then cover and return to the simmering oven for 25 minutes.

3. Whizz in a food processor, then stir in the cream and pour into individual bowls.

4. Serve with a scattering of chopped parsley on top.

chunky vegetable soup

To feed more people – use small bowls and you can make 6 servings as a starter! Double the quantity will give 8 generous helpings, or up to 12 smaller ones.

Serves 4

1 tbsp olive oil

1 onion

1 clove garlic

1 tbsp chopped fresh rosemary

1½ pints (800ml) stock

1. Peel and chop the onion, crush the garlic. Cut the carrots into even sized slices. Cut the mangetout in halves and trim and slice the spring onions.

2. Heat the oil in a heavy pan and add the carrot, onion and garlic. When sizzling, cover tightly and transfer to the simmering oven for 15 minutes until tender.

chunky vegetable soup *continued*

2 large carrots

1 tin (400g) chickpeas, drained

4 oz (110g) mangetout peas

4 spring onions

Oven:

Simmering oven, 130C, 250F, Gas 1

Prepare in advance:

Cooked, cooled soup will keep in the fridge for 24 hours

Prepare ahead:

Keep warm for half an hour in the simmering oven

Freeze: *Yes*

3 Add the rosemary, stock and chickpeas to the pan, bring to the boil and then add the mangetout and spring onions. Season well.

4 (This bit is optional, you can happily serve the soup just as it is). Whizz about half of the soup, then add the remaining half to the pan – it will be slightly thicker but still have big chunks of vegetables in it.

fish chowder

To feed more people: Double the quantity will feed at least 10, three times the quantity will fill up to 16 starter-sized soup bowls!

Serves 4

4 rashers smoked bacon

1 lb (450g) white fish

1 lb (450g) potatoes

1 onion

2 oz (55g) butter

1 tbsp plain flour

1 pint (550ml) milk

Salt and pepper

½ pint (300ml) single cream

1 tbsp chopped parsley

Oven:

Simmering oven, 130C, 250F, Gas 1

Prepare in advance:

Soup will keep in the fridge for up to 24 hours

Prepare ahead:

Keep warm in simmering oven for an hour

Freeze: *Yes*

1 Cut the bacon into strips or chunks. Peel and chop the onion. Cut the potatoes into ½" / 1cm dice.

2 Melt the butter in a pan on the simmering plate and add the bacon, potato and onion. When sizzling, cover and put into the simmering oven for 20 minutes to soften without colouring.

3 Transfer the pan to the simmering plate and stir in the flour, then slowly add the milk, stirring all the time. Bring to the boil, then cover and put back into the simmering oven for about half an hour.

4 Cut the fish into chunks and stir into the soup, then return the pan to the simmering oven for 5 minutes to cook the fish.

5 To serve, pour the cream into individual bowls, add a spoonful of chopped parsley then pour on the soup.

hot and sour noodle soup

To feed more people: Double the quantity will fill 4 to 6 starter-sized soup bowls. Three times the quantity will fill at least 8 to 10, but you may not want to increase the number of chillies beyond 2!

Serves 2

3/4 pint (425ml) good chicken stock

1" (2.5cm) piece fresh ginger

1 red chilli

1 clove garlic

2 tbsp lime juice

1 tbsp Thai fish sauce

3½ oz (100g) raw king prawns – thawed if frozen

1 oz (30g) fine rice noodles

Fresh coriander to serve

Oven:

Simmering oven, 130C, 250F, Gas 1

Prepare ahead:

Flavour and strain the broth but do not add prawns or noodles until just before serving.

Freeze:

Freeze the flavoured, strained broth but do not add prawns or noodles until reheated just before serving. Label the broth very carefully to avoid fiery stock mistakes in the freezer!

1 Bring the stock to the boil on the boiling plate.

2 Slice the ginger, garlic and chilli and drop them into the stock. Cover and transfer to the simmering oven for 5 minutes.

3 Add the lime juice and fish sauce, then the prawns. Bring the soup to the boil and add the noodles. Boil for a minute, stir in lots of chopped fresh coriander and serve at once.

4 You might warn people about the lumps of ginger and chilli, but it is more fun to fish them out than strain the soup!

5 *The longer the chillis are in the broth, the hotter the soup will be.*

swede and sweet potato soup

To feed more people: Double the ingredients will feed up to 12, but if served in mugs not bowls, up to 15

Serves 4–6

8 oz (225g) swede

8 oz (225g) sweet potatoes

1½ pints (800ml) stock

1 oz (25g) butter

1 medium onion

1 tbsp olive oil

2 cloves garlic

4 tbsp cream

Chopped parsley to

garnish

Oven:

Simmering oven, 250F, 130C, Gas 1

Prepare in advance:

Will keep in the fridge for up to 48 hours

Prepare ahead:

Keep warm in the simmering oven for an hour

Freeze:

Yes, before adding cream

1   Peel and finely chop the onion and garlic. Peel and dice the swede and sweet potato.

2   Melt the butter and oil together in a heavy based pan and add the onion and garlic. Stir over the heat until sizzling. Cover and put into the simmering oven for 15 minutes to soften. Add the swede and sweet potato to the cooked onions. Stir in the stock, bring to the boil then cover and return to the simmering oven for 25 minutes.

3   Whizz in a food processor, then stir in the cream and pour into individual bowls.

4   Serve with a scattering of chopped parsley on top.

frothy tomato soup

To feed more people: Double the ingredients will fill 10 smallish bowls

Serves 4

2 tbsp olive oil

1 onion

1 clove garlic

1 tbsp sun dried tomato purée

1 tin (400g) chopped tomatoes

1/2 tsp balsamic vinegar

Few basil leaves

1/4 tsp bicarbonate of soda

1 pint (550ml) milk

Oven:

Simmering oven, 130C, 250F, Gas 1

Prepare in advance:

Prepared soup will keep in fridge for 24 hours

Prepare ahead:

Keep warm in simmering oven for up to an hour

Freeze: *Yes*

1   Peel and chop the onion and crush the garlic.

2   Heat the oil in a pan on the simmering plate and add the onion and garlic. When sizzling, cover and transfer to the simmering oven for 15 minutes until the onions are soft.

3   Transfer the pan to the simmering plate and add the tomato purée, vinegar, tin of tomatoes and basil. Bring to the boil on the boiling plate then once again cover and transfer to the simmering oven for 15 minutes.

4   Put the bicarbonate of soda into a processor bowl with a couple of spoonsful of the milk and stir around, then add the rest of the milk.

5   Pour in the tomato mixture and whizz to a purée, then reheat until the soup stops frothing, then serve with a few more basil leaves on top.

carrot and cumin soup

To feed more people: Double the quantity will fill 10 starter-sized bowls of soup

Serves 4

12 oz (375g) carrots

8 oz (225g) potatoes

1½ pints (800ml) stock

1 oz (25g) butter

1 medium onion

1 tsp ground cumin

1 tbsp olive oil

2 cloves garlic

4 tbsp cream

Chopped parsley to garnish

Oven:

Simmering oven, 130C, 250F, Gas 1

Prepare in advance:

Will keep in the fridge for up to 48 hours

Prepare ahead:

Keep warm in the simmering oven for an hour

Freeze:

Yes, before adding cream

1   Peel and finely chop the onion and garlic. Dice the carrots and potatoes.

2   Melt the butter and oil together in a heavy based pan and add the onion and garlic. Stir over the heat until sizzling. Cover and put into the simmering oven for 15 minutes to soften. Add the carrots, potatoes and cumin to the cooked onions. Stir in the stock, bring to the boil then cover and return to the simmering oven for 25 minutes.

3   Whizz in a food processor or with a hand blender, then stir in the cream and pour into individual bowls.

4   Serve with a scattering of chopped parsley on top.

To serve a crowd, put the cream and parsley into the bowls well in advance then pour on the soup from a jug. Instant garnish and no mess before you take it to the table!

Ring the changes: try using a spoonful of grated galangal (Thai ginger) instead of the cumin.

bean and rosemary soup with pepper purée

To feed more people: Double the ingredients will make 10 bowls of soup.

Serves 4

1 carrot

1 onion

2 cloves garlic

2 tbsp olive oil

1 can (300g) cannellini beans

2 sprigs fresh rosemary or 1 tbsp dried rosemary

1³/₄ pints (1 litre) stock

Salt and pepper

1 red pepper

Oven:

Simmering oven, 130C, 250F, Gas 1

Prepare in advance:

Cooked, cooled soup will keep in the fridge for 24 hours

Prepare ahead:

Keep warm in simmering oven for an hour

Freeze:

Yes

1 Peel and chop the onion, chop the carrot and crush the garlic.

2 Heat the oil in a heavy based pan on the simmering plate and add the vegetables. Stir over the heat until they are sizzling, then cover and put into the simmering oven for 10 minutes to soften.

3 Halve the pepper and put it into a shallow roasting tin lined with Bake-O-Glide. Set the tin on the second runners in the roasting oven for 10 minutes or so until the skin is charred. Put the cooked pepper into a plastic bag and leave to cool.

4 Transfer the pan of vegetables to the boiling plate.

5 Drain the can of beans and add to the pan, with the rosemary and stock. Season and bring to the boil. Cover and put into the simmering oven for 15–20 minutes.

6 Whizz the soup in a processor and return to the pan to keep warm until needed.

7 Peel the cooled pepper and purée it in a processor – don't bother to wash the bowl after whizzing the soup!

8 Put a spoonful of pepper purée into each bowl, and then pour on the soup. Stir each bowl then serve.

green summer soup

To feed more people: Double the quantity will fill 10 starter-sized soup bowls.

Serves 4

1 tbsp olive oil

2 onions

2 cloves garlic

1 round lettuce

1 lb (450g) fresh podded (or frozen) peas

1/2 tsp sugar

1 1/2 pints (800ml) stock

Salt and pepper

1/4 pint (150ml) cream

1 pack (75g) Parma ham

Handful fresh chives

Oven:

Simmering oven, 130C, 250F, Gas 1

Prepare in advance:

Cooked, cooled soup will keep in the fridge for 24 hours

Prepare ahead:

Keep warm in simmering oven for an hour

Freeze:

Yes

1 Peel and chop the onions and crush the garlic. Slice the lettuce. Separate the ham slices and slice them into 1"/2cm strips.

2 Heat the oil in a heavy based pan on the simmering plate and add the onion and garlic. Stir over the heat until they are sizzling, then cover and put into the simmering oven for 15 minutes to soften.

3 Transfer the pan to the boiling plate and add the peas, lettuce and stock. Bring to the boil, season and simmer for about 2 minutes.

4 Whizz the soup in a processor and return to the pan to keep warm until needed.

5 Put the slices of ham into a wide frying pan and set it on the simmering plate. Shake it about occasionally as the ham fries and crisps.

6 Put a spoonful of cream and a few snipped chives into each bowl, and then pour on the soup. Stir each bowl then serve with the crisp ham on top.

roasted vegetable soup

To feed more people: Double the quantity will stretch to 10 portions, or more if served in cups rather than bowls!

Serves 4

2 red onions

2 cloves garlic

2 red peppers

1 medium potato

1 lb (450g) tomatoes

2 tbsp olive oil

1½ pints (800ml) stock or water

1 tbsp Jamaican Jerk seasoning

1 tub (200ml) crème fraîche

Salt and pepper

Handful fresh basil

Oven:

Roasting oven, 200C, 400F, Gas 6 and simmering oven, 130C, 250F, Gas 1

Prepare in advance:

Cooked, cooled soup will keep in fridge for 2 days

Prepare ahead:

Keep warm in simmering oven for an hour or so

Freeze:

Yes

1   Peel and roughly chop the onions and garlic. Trim and slice the pepper and potato into even sized chunks. Halve the tomatoes.

2   Tip the vegetables into a shallow roasting tin and pour over the oil. Shake the tin to coat the vegetables in the oil, then hang the tin from the 2nd runners in the roasting oven. Roast for about half an hour.

3   Add the stock or water and jerk seasoning to the tin, bring to the boil in the floor of the roasting oven, then cover with foil and transfer to the simmering oven for half an hour or so.

4   Pour the soup into a blender with the basil and whizz, then stir in the crème fraîche. Reheat without boiling, season to taste and serve with crusty bread.

chickpea and chorizo salad

To feed more people: Double the ingredients will feed up to 10 people as a starter, with lots of crusty bread.

Serves 4

4 oz (110g) piece chorizo sausage

1 clove garlic

2 tbsp olive oil

1 tin (400g) chickpeas

1 small red onion

1 red pepper

4" (10cm) piece cucumber

Handful fresh mint leaves

Handful fresh coriander

Handful fresh parsley

2 tbsp red wine vinegar

1 lemon

Oven:

Simmering plate

Prepare in advance:

If serving cold, complete salad will keep in fridge for up to 24 hours

Prepare ahead:

Cook chorizo and mix salad together (do not add the herbs until just before serving as they will go yellow/brown with the vinegar and heat combined) then stand beside the Aga for up to an hour before serving tepid

Freeze: *No*

1 Cut the chorizo into ½"/1cm chunks. Peel and crush the garlic. Open the tin of chickpeas and drain.

2 Heat the oil in a large sauté pan on the simmering plate and add the chorizo chunks and garlic. Shake the pan from time to time and cook for about 3–5 minutes.

3 While the sausage is cooking, slice the onion and pepper thinly and cut the cucumber into small cubes – about the size of a chickpea.

4 Grate the rind of the lemon and squeeze the juice. Chop all the herbs together.

5 Tip the chickpeas, onion and pepper into the pan and toss over the heat for a minute of two, then remove from the heat and add the lemon rind and juice, vinegar, cucumber and herbs. Season well and toss together before serving.

Variations:

• To serve the salad cold, just toss everything together and omit the Aga completely!

• To add a bit of extra oomph to the already spicy chorizo, add a chopped chilli with the onions

avocado, prawn and mango salad

To feed more people: Double the ingredients will make a starter for up to 15, carefully divided between the plates.

Serves 4 for lunch with bread, 6 as a starter

2 medium avocados

1 large mango

8 oz (225g) raw prawns

1 bag (500g) baby spinach leaves

Large handful fresh coriander

Dressing:

5 tbsp olive oil

1 tbsp lemon juice

1 tbsp cider vinegar

½ tsp sugar

Salt and pepper

Oven:

Boiling plate

Prepare in advance:

Cook the prawns, prepare and add the fruit in the dressing and refrigerate for up to 24 hours – but make sure you serve this at room temperature.

Prepare ahead:

Will sit on its plates for up to half an hour, add the coriander just before you eat it.

Freeze: *No*

1 Make the dressing: Mix all the ingredients together, in a jam jar with a lid is the easiest!

2 Chop the coriander but don't add it until just before serving, as the leaves turn brown in the vinegar.

3 Bring a pan of water to the boil and drop the prawns into it. When they turn pink – about a minute – they are cooked. Drain and tip into a bowl. Add a tablespoon of the dressing and mix well – as they cool, they will absorb the flavour of the dressing.

4 Wash and dry the spinach, then tip into a bowl and add about half of the dressing. Toss together and divide the spinach between 6 plates.

5 Halve the avocados, remove the stones then quarter them lengthways – this makes removing the skins very easy. Cut the quarters unto chunks. Put into a bowl with the rest of the dressing. Peel the mango, chop it into chunks and add to the avocado. Add the prawns and mix well.

6 Pile the fruit and prawn mixture onto the spinach leaves, divide the prawns between the plates, scatter with lots of chopped coriander and serve at once with some crusty bread.

Ring the changes:

• Substitute chunks of white fish instead of the prawns

• Substitute chunks of quorn instead of the prawns for a vegetarian version

• Substitute chunks of cooked chicken and tarragon instead of the prawns and coriander

summer vegetable salad

To feed more people: Double the quantity should feed up to 16 as part of a larger buffet.

Serves 6–8

8 oz (225g) French beans

8 oz (225g) small courgettes

8 oz (225g) sugar snap peas

Bag mixed salad leaves

Dressing:

4 tbsp olive oil

2 tbsp lemon juice

Salt and pepper

¼ tsp soft brown sugar

1 tbsp chopped fresh parsley

1 tbsp chopped fresh mint

1 tbsp chopped chives

Oven:

Boiling plate

Prepare in advance:

Cook and cool the vegetables and mix the dressing and keep in fridge for 24 hours, but do not assemble until just before eating

Prepare ahead:

Eat within an hour of assembling

Freeze:

No

1 Trim the beans and sugar snaps and cut the courgettes into halves then quarters lengthways, so that they are the same shape and size as the other vegetables.

2 Fill a large bowl with very cold water.

3 Pile all the vegetables into a pan and fill the kettle. Bring the kettle to the boil on the boiling plate, and pour boiling water over the vegetables in the pan. Set on the boiling plate and allow to boil for about a minute, then drain.

4 Tip the drained vegetables into the cold water then drain again and refill the bowl with more very cold water. Put the vegetables into that and swirl about until they are completely cold. Drain thoroughly and pat dry in a clean towel.

5 Mix the dressing ingredients together – in a jam jar is easiest.

6 Put the vegetables, salad leaves and dressing into a serving bowl and toss together before serving.

pepper and aubergine salad

To feed more people: Double the quantity will feed 14 as a starter or accompaniment to a buffet

Serves 6–8

4 red peppers

2 cloves garlic

2 aubergines

2 tbsp olive oil

1 tsp balsamic vinegar

Salt and pepper

Chopped parsley to garnish

Oven:

Aga roasting oven, 200C, 400F, Gas 6

Prepare in advance:

Prepared salad will keep in fridge for up to 24 hours

Prepare ahead:

24 hours

Freeze:

No

1 Put the peppers and unpeeled garlic into the small roasting tin and hang from the second runners in the roasting oven for about 20 minutes, until the peppers are blackened.

2 Put a ridged grill pan into the roasting oven to heat up – cast iron takes up to 10 minutes, cast aluminium (with removable handle!) about 5 minutes.

3 When the peppers are cooked, tip them into a bowl and cover with cling film to steam – this loosens the skins.

4 Slice the aubergines into thick slices. Set the hot grill pan onto the boiling plate and cook the slices of aubergine for about 5 minutes, turning once. They should have dark brown lines from the ridged pan. Cook in batches until all are ready.

5 Leave the aubergines on a wire rack to cool.

6 Peel the skins for the peppers, pull out the stalks and remove the pips. Cut into slices about the size of a finger.

7 Squeeze the flesh out of the roasted garlic cloves and put into a jar with the oil, vinegar and seasoning. Tighten the lid and shake to mix.

8 Arrange the aubergine and pepper slices in a dish and pour over the dressing. Scatter with chopped parsley and serve at room temperature.

green pea and mint salad

To feed more people: Double the ingredients will feed 10 as a starter

Serves 4, or 8 if part of a buffet

1/2 lb (225g) frozen peas

1/2 lb (225g) sugar snap peas

Handful fresh mint

7 oz (200g block) feta cheese

Bag of mixed salad leaves

Dressing:

1 tbsp runny honey

1 tbsp Dijon mustard

2 tbsp lemon juice

4 tbsp olive oil

Oven:

Boiling plate

Prepare in advance:

Assemble the dish and refrigerate for up to 4 hours before dressing and serving.

Freeze:

No

1 For the dressing: Put all the ingredients into a jam jar, put on the lid and shake well.

2 Put the peas and sugar snaps into a large saucepan. Bring the kettle to the boil and pour boiling water over the peas. Set the pan on the boiling plate until it comes back to the boil.

3 Once boiling, drain the peas into a colander, and plunge them into a bowl of cold water. Drain again and plunge them into fresh cold water. Drain again and pat dry on a tea towel if you can be bothered!

4 Chop the feta into 1/2 inch/1 cm chunks.

5 Pile the salad leaves into a bowl, add the drained peas, the feta and then scatter some chopped mint over.

6 Just before serving, pour over the dressing and toss well.

irish onion salad

To feed more people: Double the quantity will produce a bowl of salad big enough for up to 15, if served as an accompaniment to cold meat etc.

Serves 6 plus: can be served tepid, chilled or warm.

1lb (450g) tiny onions or ordinary onions cut into chunks through the root

12 fl oz (350ml) water

4 fl oz (100ml) white wine vinegar

1 tbsp olive oil

2 tbsp caster sugar

2 tbsp sun dried tomato purée

1 bay leaf

1 sprig thyme

1 sprig parsley

3 oz (85g) raisins

Salt and pepper

Freeze:

No

1 Tie the parsley and thyme together so they don't escape in the pan.

2 Peel and trim the onions – if using large ones, cut down through the root so they hold together.

3 Put all the ingredients into a heavy pan and bring to the boil. Cover and put into the simmering oven for about an hour until tender.

4 Remove the pan from the oven, remove the lid and transfer it to the floor of the roasting oven for about 20 minutes, to reduce and thicken the sauce.

irish onion salad *continued*

Oven:
Simmering oven, 130C, 250F,
Gas 1

5   Take out the herbs and serve the onions with pâté or
leftover cold turkey or ham.

Prepare in advance:
Keep in the fridge for up to 3 weeks in a sealed jar

Prepare ahead:
Keep warm beside the Aga for a couple of hours

warm pea and potato salad

Serves 4

1 lb (450g) small new potatoes

4 oz (110g) frozen peas

2 tbsp olive oil

1 tbsp lemon juice

1 tsp cumin seeds

Salt and pepper

6 quails' eggs

Oven:

Simmering oven, 130C, 250F,

Gas 1

Prepare in advance:

Make the salad, cool and

refrigerate for up to 24 hours, but

serve at room temperature or

warmed in the simmering oven for

half an hour

Prepare ahead:

Cook and assemble the salad and

serve at room temperature within

2 hours

Freeze:

No

1   Put the potatoes into a pan and cover with cold water.
Put a lid on the pan. Bring to the boil and when the
potatoes are boiling hard, drain off all the water, replace
the lid and put the pan into the simmering oven for
about half an hour until the potatoes are tender.

2   Put another pan of water on to boil and, when
bubbling, add the eggs. Set the timer for 5 minutes.
Lift the cooked eggs out of the pan and pour in the
peas, which should then come up to the boil.

3   While the peas are cooking, tip the eggs into a bowl
of cold water and peel them. Doing this while they are
hot makes it much easier and faster! Cut each egg in
half lengthways.

4   Drain the peas as soon as they boil and tip them into
the pan of potatoes, then heat the oil, lemon juice,
seasoning and cumin together in the still-warm pea
cooking pan (this saves a bit of washing up!).

5   Swirl over the heat then add to the pan of potatoes
and peas. Add the eggs. Toss together and serve
warm or tepid.

creamy asparagus tarts

To feed more people, just make more tarts. If you leave the pastry whole and make a large tart, it will feed 6 as a starter, 4 for lunch.

Serves 4

1 x pack (375g) ready rolled puff pastry

½ tub (100g) mascarpone

1 lb (450g) asparagus spears

Handful fresh basil leaves

Salt and pepper

1 lemon

2 oz (55g) Parmesan cheese

2 tbsp olive oil

Oven:

Floor of roasting oven, 200C, 400F, Gas 6

Prepare in advance:

Assemble the tarts and refrigerate until ready to bake

Prepare ahead:

Serve tepid – put beside the Aga to keep warm(ish) for up to an hour

Freeze:

No, the asparagus goes horribly soggy and the pastry goes fatty!

1 Set the mascarpone on the back of the Aga to soften.

2 Unroll the pastry and cut into four rectangles. Lay these on a piece of Bake-O-Glide, on the plain shelf.

3 Spread the mascarpone over the pastry pieces, leaving a border of about 1"/2cms around the edges. Grate the lemon rind over the mascarpone and season with salt and pepper. Tear up the basil leaves and scatter them over the top.

4 Trim the asparagus to the size of the pastry pieces (or trim the pastry to fit the asparagus!) and put the asparagus onto the pastry, dividing it evenly between the pastry pieces.

5 Using a potato peeler or large grater, shave half of the Parmesan over the asparagus.

6 Brush the edges of the pastry with olive oil and dribble the rest of the oil over the tarts.

7 Put the shelf onto the floor of the roasting oven and bake for about 15 minutes until golden, with the rest of the Parmesan shaved on top.

To ring the changes, make one large tart with the whole sheet of pastry and arrange the asparagus in a lattice then put halved cherry tomatoes and chunks of courgettes into the squares – a red and green chessboard!

lentil and vegetable stir fry

This is a lovely mixture, with the firm, nutty lentils and crunchy vegetables. It is nice as a vegetarian main dish, or to accompany sausages at a barbecue.

To feed more people: Double the quantity will make enough for about 10, or more if served to accompany another main dish.

Serves 4

8 oz (225g) firm lentils, eg. black or Puy

1 medium onion

1 clove garlic

1 tbsp olive oil

3/4 pint (450ml) stock or water

4 oz (110g) sugar snap peas

1 red pepper

1 medium courgette

4 oz (110g) baby sweetcorn

1 tbsp olive oil

2 tbsp balsamic vinegar

Salt and pepper

Oven:

Simmering oven, 130C, 250F, Gas 1

Prepare in advance:

Cooked, cooled dish will keep in fridge for 24 hours

Prepare ahead:

Keep warm in simmering oven for half an hour

Freeze:

No, the vegetables go soggy as they defrost

1   Peel and chop the onion, crush the garlic. Put into a pan with the oil and heat until sizzling. Add the lentils and stock, bring to the boil then cover and transfer to the simmering oven for about half an hour until tender.

2   Cut the vegetables into even sized pieces. Heat a large pan on the simmering plate, then transfer to the boiling plate and stir fry the vegetables for a couple of minutes until they are bright green (and red and yellow!).

3   Tip the vegetables into the cooked lentils, stir in the balsamic vinegar and season well.

4   Serve hot, warm or tepid.

aubergine and lentil daal

This is a lovely vegetarian main course, or it makes a delicious accompaniment to a curry or grilled chicken!

To feed more people: This will serve up to 8 as part of a larger curry meal, or double the quantity will go round up to 15.

Serves 4

8 oz (225g) red lentils

1 large onion

2 cloves garlic

2 tbsp sunflower oil

1 pint (550ml) stock

1"/2cms piece fresh ginger

2 tsp garam masala

1/2 tsp salt

1 medium aubergine

2 medium courgettes

4 oz (110g) cherry tomatoes

1 tbsp chopped fresh coriander

Oven:

Simmering oven, 130C, 250F, Gas 1 and boiling plate

Prepare in advance:

Cooked, cooled daal will keep in the fridge for up to 48 hours: the flavour improving as it matures

Prepare ahead:

Will keep warm in simmering oven for up to an hour

Freeze:

No, the vegetables go rubbery as they defrost

1   Peel and chop the onion, crush the garlic and peel and chop the ginger.

2   Heat the oil in a heavy pan and add the onion, garlic and ginger. Stir over the heat and, once sizzling, cover and transfer to the simmering oven for about 10 minutes to soften.

3   Wash the aubergine and courgettes and cut them into slices about 1/4"/1/2 cm across.

4   Heat a ridged grill pan in the roasting oven (cast aluminium heats up in 5 minutes, cast iron may take up to 10 minutes). Transfer the hot pan to the boiling plate and lay in the slices of aubergine and courgettes, a few at a time. Grill the slices for about 5 minutes each side, turning once.

5   Set the grilled vegetables onto a cooling rack to allow the steam to disperse.

6   Take the pan of onions from the oven, transfer to the simmering plate and stir in the garam masala and salt. Fry briefly to release the flavours, then add the lentils and stock. Bring to the boil then cover and put into the simmering oven for about 15–20 minutes.

7   Cut the tomatoes into halves and chop the coriander. Cut the slices of aubergine and courgettes into quarters. When the lentils are cooked, stir in the aubergine, courgettes, tomatoes and coriander and serve.

spinach and blue cheese tart

To feed more people: Double the quantity will fill a 12"/30cms flan dish and should serve up to 14 people.

Serves 4–6

6 oz (175g) plain flour

3 oz (75g) butter

2 tbsp Parmesan cheese

1 tbsp poppy seeds

2-3 tbsp water

4 oz (110g) Stilton cheese, crumbled

8 oz (225g) spinach

3 eggs

5 fl oz (150ml) milk

Salt and pepper

Oven:

Roasting oven, 200C, 400F, Gas 6

Prepare ahead:

Cooked cooled tart will keep in the fridge for up to 24 hours, although it is nicer on the day it is baked!

Prepare in advance:

Tart will keep warm in the simmering oven for half an hour

Freeze:

Yes, uncooked pastry

1   To make the pastry, put the flour, butter, poppy seeds and Parmesan into a processor and whizz until the texture of breadcrumbs. With the motor running, add the water a spoonful at a time until it comes together as a dough.

2   Roll out the pastry and line a 9"/23cm flan dish. Chill or freeze until required.

3   For the filling, wash the spinach and put into a large pan. Set the pan onto the simmering plate for about 5 minutes, until the spinach has wilted. Drain thoroughly and press out as much water as possible. Spread the spinach over the base of the pastry case, then scatter over the Stilton.

4   Mix the eggs and milk with a little salt and pepper and beat together.

5   Pour into the prepared flan case and put onto the floor of the roasting oven for about 25 minutes until set and golden.

21st century macaroni cheese

To feed more people: Double the quantity will give 8–10 portions.

Serves 4

6 oz (175g) macaroni

1 onion

1 oz (25g) plain flour

1 oz (25g) butter

3/4 pint (450ml) milk

2 eggs

3 oz (75g) mascarpone

2 oz (55g) gruyère cheese

1 oz (25g) fresh Parmesan

Oven:

Grid shelf on floor of roasting oven

190C, 375F, Gas 5

Prepare in advance:

Assemble the dish and refrigerate for up to 4 hours before final cooking

Prepare ahead:

Keep warm in the simmering oven for up to half an hour

Freeze:

Yes, cooked

1   Grate the gruyère. Grate the Parmesan into a separate bowl. Set the mascarpone on the back of the Aga to soften. Separate the eggs.

2   Melt the butter in a pan on the simmering plate, add the onions and when sizzling, transfer to the simmering oven for 10 minutes to soften.

3   Cook the macaroni in boiling water according to the instructions on the packet. Drain.

4   Remove onions from the oven and stir in the flour and then the milk. Gently bring to the boil, stirring all the time.

5   Remove sauce from the heat and beat in the egg yolks and the warm mascarpone and grated gruyère.

6   Whisk the egg whites and fold them into the sauce. Fold in the cooked pasta and pour into an ovenproof dish. Scatter the grated Parmesan over the top and bake for about 25 minutes until browned and bubbling.

pissaladière

For a vegetarian pissaladière, leave out the anchovies

To feed more people: Double the quantity will fill a 12"/30cms flan dish and should give at least 12 portions.

Serves 4–6

For the pastry:

6 oz (175g) plain flour

3 oz (85g) butter

1 tbsp Parmesan cheese

2-3 tbsp water

For the filling:

1 lb (450g) onions

2 cloves garlic

2 tomatoes

1 tin (85g) anchovy fillets

about 15 stoned black olives

1 tbsp olive oil

Salt and pepper

Oven:

Aga roasting oven, 200C, 400F, Gas 6

Prepare ahead:

24 hours

Freeze:

Yes

1 To make the pastry, put the flour, butter and Parmesan into a processor and whizz until the texture of breadcrumbs. With the motor running, add the water a spoonful at a time until it comes together as a dough.

2 Roll out the pastry and line a 9"/23cm flan dish. Chill or freeze until required.

3 For the filling: Peel and slice the onions and crush the garlic. Put into a heavy based pan with the olive oil and heat on the boiling plate until sizzling. Cover and transfer to the simmering oven for about 20 minutes to soften.

4 Roughly chop the tomatoes and add them to the onions – mix together. Put the pan onto the floor of the roasting oven to reduce for about 5 minutes. Remove from the oven and allow to cool a little.

5 Pour the onion mixture into the prepared flan case. Lay the anchovy fillets in a lattice pattern over the onions and put an olive into each 'diamond' space.

6 Put the tart onto the floor of the roasting oven for about 25 minutes until the pastry is golden.

risotto alla milanese

To feed more people: Double the quantity will feed 8, or 10 as a starter.

Serves 4

8 oz (half a pint in a measuring jug) (225g) risotto rice

1 medium onion

2 cloves garlic

2 tbsp olive oil

1 oz (25g) butter

1 pint (550ml) stock

2 tbsp white wine

Salt and pepper

3 tbsp grated Parmesan cheese

Parsley to garnish

Oven:

Simmering oven, 130C, 250F, Gas 1

Prepare in advance

Cooked, cooled risotto will keep in fridge for 24 hours

Prepare ahead:

Will keep warm for a couple of hours in the simmering oven

Freeze:

Yes, defrost and reheat in roasting oven for half an hour

1   Peel and chop the onion, crush the garlic.

2   Heat the oil and butter in a heavy pan on the simmering plate, and add the onion and garlic. When sizzling, cover and put into the simmering oven for 15 minutes to soften.

3   Stir the rice into the cooked onions, add the wine and stock to the pan. Bring to the boil, then cover and return to the simmering oven for at least 30 minutes.

4   Stir the Parmesan into the risotto, then serve with a scattering of chopped parsley.

courgette tart

To feed more people: Double the ingredients will fill a 12"/30cms tart case, or make two tarts to serve up to 12 people.

Serves 4–6

For the pastry:

6 oz (175g) plain flour

3 oz (75g) butter

2 tbsp Parmesan cheese

1 tbsp onion seeds

2–3 tbsp water

For the filling:

2 medium courgettes

1 tbsp olive oil

1 clove garlic

3 eggs

5 fl oz (150ml) milk

4 oz (110g) cheddar cheese

1 tbsp Dijon mustard

Salt and pepper

Oven:

Roasting oven, 200C, 400F, Gas 6

Prepare ahead:

Make the pastry case and chill for 24 hours before filling and cooking.

Freeze:

Yes

1 To make the pastry, put the flour, butter, onion seeds and Parmesan into a processor and whizz until the texture of breadcrumbs. With the motor running, add the water a spoonful at a time until it comes together as a dough.

2 Roll out the pastry and line a 9"/23cm flan dish. Chill or freeze until required.

3 For the filling, grate the cheese and keep on one side. Grate the courgettes and crush the garlic. Put them into a heavy based pan and set onto the boiling plate. Stir fry for 2–3 minutes until bright green in colour and steaming, to boil off some of the liquid they contain. Remove from the heat and tip into the pastry case, with the grated cheese.

4 Mix the eggs and milk with the mustard and a little salt and pepper and beat together.

5 Pour into the prepared flan case and put onto the floor of the roasting oven for about 25 minutes until set and golden.

potato and chickpea curry

To feed more people: this quantity will give up to 8 servings if served as part of a larger curry spread. Double the quantity will give 8 proper portions!

Serves 4

12 oz (375g) potatoes

2 onions

2 cloves garlic

1 tbsp vegetable oil

1 tsp ground coriander

1 tsp ground turmeric

1 tsp smoked paprika

1 tsp ground cumin

½ tsp salt

1 tin (400g) chickpeas, drained

2 tbsp sun dried tomato purée

½ pint (300ml) vegetable stock or water

8 oz (200g pack) spinach

2 tbsp chopped fresh coriander

Oven:

Simmering oven, 130C, 250F, Gas 1

Prepare in advance:

Cooked, cooled curry will keep in fridge for 24 hours

Prepare ahead:

Keep warm in simmering oven for up to an hour

Freeze:

Yes

1 Cut the potatoes into chunks about 3/4"/2cm across.

2 Put the potatoes into a large pan, cover with cold water and bring to the boil. When boiling hard, drain off all the water, cover tightly and put into the simmering oven for about 25 minutes until tender.

3 Peel and chop the onions, crush the garlic. Heat the oil in a heavy sautée pan or casserole and add the onions and garlic. When sizzling, cover and put into the simmering oven for about 15 minutes until softened.

4 When the onions have softened, stir in the spices and salt and fry for a minute to release their flavour. Stir in the chickpeas, tomato purée and water, and add the potatoes once they are cooked.

5 Boil the pan hard, then tip in the spinach. Stir until it has wilted a little, then serve with the coriander scattered over the top.

onion bhajis

To feed more people: Double the mixture will fry in the same amount of oil and will make 20, or 24 smaller, bhajis

Makes about 10

2 large onions

4 oz (110g) plain flour

1 tsp ground cumin

1 tsp ground coriander

½ tsp turmeric

½ tsp chilli powder

1 tsp salt

3 fl oz (75ml) water

3 tbsp chopped fresh coriander

Sunflower oil for frying

Oven:

Boiling plate

Prepare in advance:

Either keep the uncooked bhajis in the fridge for up to 24 hours before cooking, or cook, chill and reheat in roasting oven.

Prepare ahead:

Fry the bhajis, allow to cool then reheat in roasting oven for 5 minutes

Freeze:

Uncooked bhajis

1 Peel the onions.

2 Put them into the bowl of a processor, with all the other ingredients. Whizz to a paste.

3 Put a heavy pan onto the simmering plate and fill with 2"/5cms of oil. Allow to heat up for about 5 minutes, then transfer to the boiling plate.

4 The oil is hot enough when a teaspoon of the mixture will rise to the surface when dropped in.

5 Using two spoons, scoop the mixture into balls and gently drop them into the oil. If they are cooking too fast, move the pan to the simmering plate. Turn the bhajis once in the oil to brown all over.

6 The bhajis are cooked when they are golden brown.

7 Lift out of the oil onto a sheet of kitchen paper before serving with raita.

cucumber raita

To feed more people: This allows for a generous helping for each of 6 people, but should be plenty for 8. Double the quantity will be more than enough for 16, to accompany a curry.

Serves 4

1 pint (550ml) yogurt

½ cucumber

2 tbsp fresh mint

½ tsp ground cumin

¼ tsp cayenne pepper

½ tsp salt

Prepare in advance:

Will keep for a day in the fridge

Freeze: *No*

1 Cut the cucumber into ½"/1cm dice.

2 Mix together all the ingredients.

daal

To feed more people: Double the quantity will feed up to 10, especially if as part of a large curry meal with other accompaniments.

Serves 4

7 oz (200g) red lentils

1 pint (550ml) water

2 slices fresh ginger

½ tsp ground turmeric

1 tsp salt

3 tbsp vegetable oil

1 tsp ground cumin

1 tsp ground coriander

½ tsp cayenne pepper

2 tbsp fresh coriander, chopped

Oven:

Simmering oven, 130C, 250F, Gas 1

Prepare in advance:

Cooked, cooled daal will keep for up to 48 hours in the fridge

Prepare ahead:

Keep warm in the simmering oven for an hour

Freeze:

Yes

1 Put the lentils, slice of ginger, turmeric and water into a heavy pan and bring to the boil. Cover and transfer to the simmering oven for about half an hour.

2 Remove the lentils from the oven, take out the slices of ginger and stir in the salt.

3 Heat the oil in a small pan and add the cumin, coriander and cayenne. Swirl over the heat for a minute, then pour into the lentils.

4 Stir together and serve with a scattering of chopped coriander.

spiced aubergines

To feed more people: This quantity will make a side dish or starter for 8 with other dishes, or double the ingredients will feed up to 15.

Serves 4

2 large aubergines

2 tbsp olive oil

1 tbsp sesame oil

2 tbsp rice vinegar

1 ball stem ginger and 2 tbsp syrup from the jar

2 tbsp soy sauce

2 spring onions

1 tsp chilli powder

1 tbsp chopped fresh coriander

Oven:

Boiling plate

Prepare in advance:

Mix the dressing and slice the aubergines up to 24 hours in advance.

Prepare ahead:

Will keep warm in the simmering oven for an hour

Freeze:

No, the aubergines go rubbery as they defrost

1   Slice the aubergines into $1/2$"/1cm slices.

2   Slice the spring onions into thinnish rounds.

3   Grate the stem ginger then add the syrup, oils, vinegar, soy sauce and chilli and mix well – easiest in a jam jar with the lid on.

4   Put a ridged grill pan into the roasting oven to heat up – cast iron will take about 10 minutes, cast aluminium will take about 5 minutes.

5   Transfer the pan to the boiling plate and add the slices of aubergine, a few at a time. Cook on the boiling plate for about 5 minutes each side, then put the cooked slices onto a cooling rack for the steam to disperse. Continue to grill the remaining slices of aubergine and allow to steam, then put them into a wide, shallow serving dish.

6   Tip the sauce ingredients into the hot pan, then pour over the aubergine slices. Scatter the coriander over and serve at once.

pasta al sugo

To feed more people: Double the quantity will feed up to 10 people, but will need a little longer on the floor of the roasting oven to reduce the larger quantity of tomatoes.

Serves 4

8 oz (225g) penne pasta

2 lb (900g) fresh tomatoes or 2 tins chopped tomatoes

1 onion

2 cloves garlic

Handful fresh basil

1 tsp caster sugar

Salt and pepper

Grated fresh Parmesan cheese

Oven:

Roasting oven

Prepare in advance:

Cooked cooled pasta sauce will keep in the fridge for 48 hours

Prepare ahead:

Sauce will keep warm in simmering oven for an hour

Freeze:

Sauce, yes

1 Peel and chop the onion, peel and crush the garlic. Heat the oil in a heavy pan on the simmering plate and add the onion and garlic. When sizzling, cover and transfer to the simmering oven for about 10 minutes, to soften.

2 Meanwhile, if using fresh tomatoes, boil the kettle and pour the water over a bowl full of tomatoes. Count to 30, then drain and fill the bowl with cold water. Peel the skins from the tomatoes and chop them.

3 When the onions have cooked, add the tomatoes, sugar, a few basil leaves and the seasoning to the pan, stir then transfer to the floor of the roasting oven to boil and reduce for about 20 minutes, until thickened.

4 Bring a large pan of water to the boil and cook the pasta according to the instructions on the packet. When cooked, drain.

5 Pour pasta into the tomato sauce pan and stir together. Serve at once, shaving some fresh Parmesan over the top and scattering with fresh basil leaves.

thai vegetable curry

To feed more people: Double the ingredients will feed 8 or 9, or more if served with lots of rice or as part of a Thai buffet.

Serves 4

1 butternut squash

1 onion

1 clove garlic

1 sachet coconut cream

½ pint (300ml) vegetable stock

4 oz (115g) mangetout peas

1 tbsp red Thai curry paste

Salt and pepper

1 tbsp chopped fresh coriander

Oven:

Simmering oven, 130C, 250F, Gas 1

Prepare in advance:

Cooked, chilled curry will keep in the fridge for up to 24 hours

Prepare ahead:

Will keep warm in simmering oven for half an hour

Freeze:

Yes

1 Peel the squash and cut it into even sized chunks, about 1"/2.5cm.

2 Peel and chop the onion, crush the garlic.

3 Heat the oil in a heavy based pan and add the squash, onion and garlic. Stir until sizzling then cover and put into the simmering oven for about 20 minutes to soften.

4 When the vegetables are soft, move the pan to the boiling plate and add the remaining ingredients.

5 Boil for a minute, scatter with chopped coriander, then serve with lots of naan bread to soak up the juices.

lentil and vegetable bake

A warm and welcoming autumn harvest supper

To feed more people: Double the quantity will give 12 generous portions, especially if served with grilled meat!

Serves 6

2 onions

1 clove garlic

1 tbsp olive oil

2 parsnips

2 medium potatoes

1 small swede

2 carrots

8 oz (225g) red lentils

1 pint (550ml) stock or water

1 tsp Jamaican jerk seasoning

Salt and pepper

4 oz (110g) grated Cheddar cheese

Oven:

Simmering oven, 130C, 250F, Gas 1 and roasting oven, 200C, 400F, Gas 6

Prepare in advance:

Cooked, cooled casserole will keep in fridge for up to 24 hours

Prepare ahead:

Keep warm in simmering oven for up to an hour

Freeze:

Yes

1 Peel and chop the onion and garlic. Cut the parsnips, potatoes, swede and carrots into even sized chunks.

2 Heat the oil in a heavy based pan on the simmering plate and add the vegetables. Stir around and once sizzling, cover and transfer to the simmering oven.

3 Take pan of vegetables from the oven and stir in the lentils and season well. Pour on the stock or water, and bring to the boil on the boiling plate then cover the pan and return it to the simmering oven for about half an hour. Or an hour. Or two hours, until you are ready to eat it.

4 Remove the lid from the pan, scatter the cheese over the top of the lentil bake and set on the grid shelf high in the roasting oven for about 5–10 minutes until the cheese is melted and golden.

5 Serve with a green vegetable.

mushroom salad gougère

To feed more people: Double the quantity will make two large or three slightly smaller gougères, each serving 4 people.

Serves 4

¼ pint (150ml) water

2 oz (55g) butter

2½ oz (65g) plain flour

2 eggs

2 oz (55g) grated Cheddar

3 tbsp mayonnaise

4 oz chestnut mushrooms

3 spring onions

1 tsp sun dried tomato purée

Juice ½ lime

2 tbsp fresh coriander

salt and pepper

Oven:

Roasting oven, 200C, 400F, Gas 6

Prepare ahead:

1 hour

Freeze:

Yes, gougère ring only

1   Put the water and butter into a heavy based pan and slowly bring to the boil on the simmering plate. When it is boiling, tip in the flour and beat well. Break in the eggs one at a time and beat well, then beat in half of the grated cheese.

2   Line the plain shelf with Bake-O-Glide and then spoon blobs of the mixture into a circle on the sheet. Sprinkle over the remaining grated cheese. Hang the shelf from the third set of runners in the roasting oven and bake for 25–30 minutes until the pastry is golden and puffed up. Remove from the oven and allow to cool before sliding onto a plate.

3   Cut the mushrooms into quarters and trim and slice the spring onions.

4   Mix the mayonnaise, lime juice and tomato purée together. Tip in the mushrooms and onions, stir together then pile into the centre of the gougère. Scatter over the chopped coriander and serve with a tomato salad and some crusty bread.

spiced mashed potatoes

To feed more people: Double the quantity will feed up to 8, 10 if you serve people rather than them helping themselves!

Serves 4

1½ lb (750g) floury potatoes

2 tsp turmeric

½ tsp salt

Small tub (100ml) natural yogurt

1 tbsp korma paste

Bunch spring onions

Oven:

Simmering oven, 130C, 250F, Gas 1

Prepare in advance:

Mashed potatoes will keep in fridge for up to 48 hours

Prepare ahead:

Keep warm in simmering oven for up to an hour – leave the potatoes in their pan after mashing and pour over about 3 tbsp milk. Stir this into the mash before serving

Freeze: *Yes*

1　Cut the potatoes into even sized chunks.

2　Put the potato chunks into a pan and cover with cold water. Bring to the boil and, once boiling hard, drain off all the water, cover tightly and put into the simmering oven for about 30 minutes until tender.

3　While the potatoes are in the oven, mix together the turmeric, salt, yogurt and paste in a bowl and set it on the back of the Aga to warm up.

4　Trim and slice the spring onions.

5　Once the potatoes are cooked, mash them with the spicy, yellow yogurt and stir in the spring onions.

6　Serve with sausages or tamarind chicken.

mashed sweet potato
and celeriac

This is delicious with roasted meat and roast potatoes. If there is any left over, add a pint of stock and you have a garlicky, herby vegetable soup!

To feed more people: Double the ingredients will feed up to 10 if served with other vegetables as an accompaniment

Serves 4

1 lb (450g) sweet potatoes

1 lb (450g) celeriac

1 pack (250g) garlic and herb cream cheese

Salt and pepper

Oven:

Simmering oven, 130C, 250F, Gas 1

Prepare in advance: Cooked, cooled mash will keep in the fridge for 24 hours

Prepare ahead:

Will keep warm for up to an hour

Freeze: *Yes*

1　Set the cream cheese on the back of the Aga to soften.

2　Peel the sweet potatoes and celeriac and cut into even sized pieces. Bring to the boil on the boiling plate, drain, cover and put into the simmering oven for 35–40 minutes until soft. Drain again.

3　Mash, then add the cream cheese, salt and pepper. Beat with a wooden spoon until smooth and serve.

crispy potato wedges

To feed more people: Double the quantity will feed 8 adults or 4 teenagers!

Serves 4

4 large floury potatoes

2 tbsp sunflower oil

Grated rind and juice of a lemon

¼ tsp smoked paprika

¼ tsp salt

½ tsp ground cumin

½ tsp chili powder (optional!)

Oven:

Roasting oven, 200C, 400F, Gas 6

Prepare in advance:

Coat the potatoes in the mix a couple of hours before cooking

Prepare ahead:

When cooked remove from oven, leave to cool then reheat for 5 minutes before serving

Freeze:

Yes, reheat in roasting oven for 15 minutes from frozen

1 Cut the potatoes into big wedge-shaped chunks. Put into a large bowl.

2 Pour on the oil and add the spices and lemon rind and juice. Mix together thoroughly.

3 Line a large shallow baking tray with Bake-O-Glide.

4 Tip the coated potatoes onto the tray and hang from the second runners in the roasting oven. Cook for about 45 minutes until crisp and golden.

5 Serve as soon as possible, perhaps with a yogurt based dip.

roasted sesame sprouts

To feed more people: Double the quantity will feed up to 10 with other vegetables as part of a Sunday lunch or Christmas dinner.

Serves 4

1 lb (450g) sprouts

2 tbsp sesame oil

Salt and pepper

2 tbsp sesame seeds

Oven:

Aga roasting oven, 400F, 200C, Gas 6

Prepare in advance:

Coated, uncooked sprouts will keep in fridge for 24 hours

Prepare ahead:

Keep warm for up to an hour, but they are nicest freshly cooked

Freeze: *No*

1 Line a small shallow baking tray with Bake-O-Glide.

2 Trim and prepare the sprouts.

3 Pile into a bowl, add the sesame seeds and oil and toss together until the sprouts are well coated. Tip into the tin.

4 Hang the tin from the second set of runners and roast for 7–10 minutes, season and serve.

chunky roasted squash

To feed more people: The same quantity will go around 8 people if served with other vegetables. Double the quantity will feed up to 16 if served with other vegetables, or 10 as a single vegetable accompaniment.

Serves 4

1 butternut squash

1 slice bread

1 clove garlic

1 red chilli

Handful fresh sage

2 tbsp olive oil

Salt and pepper

Oven:

Roasting oven, 200C, 400F, Gas 6

Prepare in advance:

Cut up and coat the squash up to 24 hours in advance

Prepare ahead:

Don't try to keep warm, allow to cool then reheat for 5 minutes at the top of the roasting oven

Freeze:

Yes, reheat straight from the freezer in the roasting oven for 15 minutes

1 Peel the squash and cut into chunks, removing all the pips and stringy pith. Tip into a large bowl. Add the oil and stir to coat the squash.

2 Put the garlic, chilli, sage and bread into a processor and whizz. Tip over the squash and shake to coat in the chilli crumbs, which will stick to the oil.

3 Line a shallow baking tray with Bake-O-Glide and tip in the coated squash.

4 Roast on the 3rd runners in the roasting oven for about 45 minutes until crispy and browned.

This works really well with any or all similar vegetables – pumpkin, parsnips, marrow, aubergine, etc.

foolproof sliced potatoes

Not quite gratin dauphinois, but a lot easier and guaranteed to work every time!

To feed more people: Double the quantity will give 12 portions, more if served as part of a buffet.

Serves 6

2lb (900g) floury potatoes

½ pint (300ml) milk

½ pint (300ml) double cream

1 onion

2 cloves garlic

Salt and pepper

2 oz (55g) butter

Oven:

Simmering oven, 130C, 250F, Gas 1 then roasting oven, 200C, 400F, Gas 6

Prepare in advance:

Assemble the dish and refrigerate for up to 4 hours before cooking

Prepare ahead:

Keep warm in the simmering oven for half an hour

Freeze:

Yes

1 Set the butter in a bowl on the back of the Aga to melt.

2 Cut the potatoes into even sized slices, about the thickness of two pound coins together. Peel and slice the onion and crush the garlic.

3 Put the potatoes, onions, garlic, milk, cream and seasoning into a wide, shallow pan. Bring to the boil on the boiling plate then cover and transfer to the simmering oven for about 40 minutes until the potatoes are soft.

4 Take the pan from the simmering oven, and remove the lid. Pour over the melted butter.

5 Set the grid shelf on the 3rd set of runners in the roasting oven and put the pan onto this and bake for about 15 minutes until browned.

credit crunch lobster

Serves 4
  4 sheets filo pastry
  2 tbsp olive oil
  1 frozen lobster, about 1lb / 450g, defrosted
  1 bunch asparagus spears

Sauce:
  1 small onion
  1 clove garlic
  1 tbsp olive oil
  ½ pint (300ml) fish stock
  1 tbsp white vermouth
  1 tbsp cornflour
  2 egg yolks
  Salt and pepper

Or, just use three tablespoons of nice mayonnaise for sauce!

Oven:
  Roasting oven, 190C, 375F, Gas 5

Prepare in advance:
  Cooked cooled cases will keep in an airtight tin for up to a week.

Prepare ahead:
  Prepare the filling and sauce in advance, but fill the cases just before serving

Freeze:
  Cooked pastry cases only

1 Stack the sheets of pastry on a flat surface and cut into quarters. Lay a plastic bag with a damp cloth inside it on top of the pastry sheets whilst you prepare each one (this stops them drying out but also prevents them going soggy as they would with a damp cloth in direct contact with the pastry).

2 Brush each piece of pastry with a little oil and arrange in a muffin tin, four layers of pastry to each of four cases. Press down in the centre to fill the muffin shape.

3 Put the muffin tin into the large roasting tin and hang from the lowest runners in the roasting oven, with the plain shelf on the second runner above. Bake for about 5 minutes until pale golden. Remove the pastry cases from the oven and transfer to a rack to cool.

4 For the sauce: Peel and chop the onion, crush the garlic. Heat the oil in a heavy pan and add the onion and garlic. Put the pan onto the simmering plate until it is sizzling, then cover and transfer to the simmering oven for about 15 minutes until the onion is soft. Take the pan from the oven and stir in the stock. Mix the vermouth with the cornflour and stir into the pan, then bring to the boil. It will thicken a little.

5 Pour the boiling sauce onto the egg yolks, whisking all the time, so that the yolks are incorporated into the sauce and it will thicken a little more – like a butterless hollandaise.

6 Cut the asparagus into 2"/5cms lengths. Bring a pan of water to the boil and drop in the asparagus. When the pan is boiling hard, drain it and tip the hot asparagus into a bowl of cold water, to set the bright green colour.

7 Bash the lobster with a rolling pin and break it up to remove all the flesh. Chop this roughly.

8 Stir the lobster meat and asparagus into the sauce and pile into the pastry cases. Serve at once, whilst it is still tepid.

Alternatives:

• Substitute half a pound (225g) of cooked, peeled prawns for the lobster
• Substitute a bag of frozen mixed seafood for the lobster, although this will probably cost about the same!
• For a vegetarian version, substitute chopped Quorn for the fish and use vegetable stock for the sauce

salmon parcels

To feed more people: Make one salmon parcel per person.

Serves 4

4 salmon steaks

4 rice flour wrappers

2 tbsp pesto sauce

Handful fresh basil leaves

2 tbsp olive oil

Oven:

Roasting oven, 200C, 400F, Gas 6

Prepare in advance:

Uncooked parcels will keep in the fridge for 24 hours

Prepare ahead:

Eat as soon as possible after cooking, as the parcels will eventually go soggy if kept warm for too long

Freeze:

Uncooked parcels

1   Fill a wide, shallow bowl with warm water.

2   Dip a rice wrapper into the water until it softens, then remove to a board. Lay a basil leaf onto the centre of the wrapper, then put a salmon steak onto the leaf. Spread about half a tablespoon of pesto over the steak, and fold the rice wrapper around the fish into a neat parcel.

3   Repeat for the remaining salmon steaks and rice wrappers.

4   Set the parcels into a shallow baking tray lined with Bake-O-Glide and brush them with the oil.

5   Hang the tin from the 3rd runners in the roasting oven and bake for about 15 minutes, until the parcels are crisp and golden.

6   Serve with a big bowl of salad.

Alternatives:

- Use white fish fillets instead of the salmon

- Try red pesto instead of the basil pesto

- Try rocket or coriander pesto instead of the basil pesto – change the fresh herb leaf according to the flavour

- Use smoked fish fillets with a spoonful of horseradish sauce instead of the pesto

- Try garlic and herb flavoured cream cheese instead of the pesto

- For a vegetarian alternative, use Quorn chicken-sized pieces in the parcels

kate ransom's steamed salmon florentine

To feed more people: Double the quantity will feed up to 12 as a starter, or 8 for a main course with salad.

Serves 4

4 salmon steaks – the cold smoked ones are particularly nice

Small tub (200g) crème fraîche

2 tbsp dill sauce

Salt and pepper

1 lb (450g) fresh spinach

Oven:

Roasting oven, 200C, 400F, Gas 6

Prepare in advance:

Assemble the dish and chill for up to 24 hours before cooking

Prepare ahead:

Keep warm in simmering oven for half an hour

Freeze:

No

1 Wash the spinach and dry thoroughly. Put into a large, ovenproof casserole.

2 Lay the salmon steaks on top of the spinach.

3 Mix the crème fraîche with the dill sauce and season well.

4 Pour this sauce over the salmon steaks then put a tight-fitting lid onto the casserole.

5 Set the grid shelf on the floor of the roasting oven and put the casserole onto it. Bake for about 20 minutes, until the spinach has wilted, the salmon is cooked and everything is coated in the creamy sauce.

6 Serve with steamed new potatoes.

smoked salmon pasta

To feed more people, use a larger casserole and double the ingredients to cook 8 salmon steaks.

Serves 4

250g (9oz) fresh linguine pasta

250g (8oz) pack smoked salmon

Small tub (200g) crème fraîche

2 tbsp dill sauce

1 lemon

Salt and pepper

1 For the sauce, set the tub of crème fraîche on the back of the Aga to warm up.

2 Cut the smoked salmon into strips. Grate the rind of the lemon and squeeze the juice.

3 Bring a large pan of water to the boil and tip in the pasta and cook for the length of time directed on the packet.

smoked salmon pasta *continued*

Oven:

    Boiling plate

Prepare in advance:

    Make the sauce and chill up to 24
    hours in advance

Prepare ahead:

    Cooked pasta in sauce will keep
    warm for up to half an hour in
    simmering oven

4   Drain the cooked pasta and tip the crème fraîche, dill sauce, lemon rind and juice, seasoning and smoked salmon into the warm pan.

5   Return the pasta to the pan and stir well. Serve at once.

Freeze:

    Don't see why not!

prawn curry

To feed more people: Double the ingredients will feed up to 10, or more if part of a large curry selection.

Serves 4

    12 oz (350g) king prawns

    12 oz (350g) courgettes

    1 tsp salt

    3 tbsp vegetable oil

    3 cloves garlic

    1 green chilli

    $1/2$ tsp turmeric

    1 tsp ground cumin

    $1/4$ tsp ground cayenne

    1 can (340g) chopped tomatoes

    $1/2$"/1cm piece fresh ginger

Oven:

    Boiling pate

Prepare ahead:

    Cook to the end of stage 5, keep
    in fridge for up to 24 hours.

Prepare in advance:

    Cook to the end of stage 5 and
    keep warm for up to half an hour

Freeze:

    No

1   Put the prawns in a sieve with some kitchen paper underneath to absorb as much of their liquid as possible.

2   Wash the courgettes and cut into $1/2$"/1cm dice.

3   Peel and crush the garlic, chop the chilli finely, peel and grate the ginger.

4   Put a wide, heavy pan into the roasting oven to heat up for 5 minutes. Transfer the pan to the boiling plate.

5   Heat the oil in the pan, then add the courgettes and stir-fry for a couple of minutes. Add the garlic, chilli and ginger and stir in, then add the dry spices, followed by the tomatoes.

6   Bring to the boil, then stir in the prawns. Boil for a minute or two and serve at once.

skate with ginger and chilli

To feed more people: each large-ish skate wing will feed two people as a main course. Double the sauce is plenty for 5 skate wings, i.e. 10 people.

Serves 4

2 skate wings, about 12 oz (325g) each

2 tbsp groundnut oil

Bunch spring onions

1"/2½ cm piece root ginger

1 clove garlic

1 small red chilli

1 tsp sun dried tomato purée

1 tbsp dark soy sauce

1 tbsp rice vinegar

1 tsp sesame oil

1 tbsp fresh coriander

Oven:

Roasting oven to heat the pan, then boiling plate

Prepare in advance:

Chop all the ingredients and keep in the fridge for up to 12 hours before cooking

Prepare ahead:

No, this is a cook and go meal!

Freeze:

No

1 Put a large, wide based heavy sauté pan into the roasting oven to heat up before you start preparing the sauce.

2 Rinse and trim the spring onions, then slice thinly. Peel and chop the ginger and garlic. Halve the chilli and remove the seeds, then chop finely. Mix together the onions, garlic, ginger and chilli.

3 Mix together the tomato purée, soy sauce, rice vinegar and sesame oil (in a jam jar is easiest).

4 Transfer the hot pan to the boiling plate and heat the groundnut oil in it.

5 Dry the skate wings on a piece of kitchen paper, then put them into the pan and fry for a couple of minutes until browned. Turn the wings over and transfer the pan to the floor of the roasting oven for a further 5 minutes.

6 When the fish is cooked, remove from the pan to a plate and keep warm. Tip the spring onion mixture into the pan and stir fry for a minute, then pour in the soy sauce mixture and stir until boiling.

7 Tip the hot sauce mixture onto the skate, chop the coriander over and eat at once.

salmon fish cakes

To feed more people: This quantity, made into one large fish cake, should go around 6 people with some salad for lunch. Double the quantity, also served as one large fishcake and cut into wedges, will give 10 portions.

Serves 4

1 lb (450g) potatoes

¼ pint (150ml) milk

1 medium onion

1 oz (25g) butter

3 cold smoked salmon fillet pieces, about 5 oz (150g) each

Grated rind and juice of a lemon

2 tbsp chopped chives

Salt and pepper

1 oz (25g) butter

2 tbsp olive oil

Oven:

Simmering oven, 130C, 250F, Gas 1 and floor of roasting oven

Prepare in advance:

Prepared fish cakes will keep in the fridge for up to 24 hours before frying

Prepare ahead:

Keep warm in simmering oven for half an hour

Freeze:

Yes, before frying. Defrost and cook as instruction, or cook from frozen for about 10 minutes each side

1 Cut up the potatoes and put into a pan. Cover with cold water, bring to a serious boil on the boiling plate then drain completely, cover the pan and put into the simmering oven for about half an hour until the potatoes are soft. Set the milk in a mug on the back of the Aga to warm.

2 Peel and chop the onion then put it into a pan with the butter and heat on the simmering plate until sizzling. Cover and transfer to the simmering oven for about 15 minutes to soften.

3 Line a small shallow baking tray with Bake-O-Glide. Lay the salmon steaks on the tray, grate over the lemon rind and sprinkle on the juice and then hang the tin from the second set of runners in the roasting oven for about 6–7 minutes. Remove from the oven once cooked and allow to cool.

4 When the potatoes are cooked, mash with the warm milk, season well.

5 Remove the skins from the salmon steaks and add the steaks to the pan of mashed potato, along with the cooked onions and chopped chives. If time allows, leave to become completely cold.

6 Stir everything together, and form into round shapes. Roll in the flour, then flatten slightly.

7 Set the fish cakes on a plate, cover and put into the fridge for half an hour, if possible, to firm up.

8 Heat the butter and oil in a heavy frying pan, add the fish cakes then transfer to the floor of the roasting oven to fry until browned – about 5 minutes. Turn the cakes and return to the oven floor to brown the underside.

9 Serve with a green vegetable.

steamed sea bass

To feed more people: The same quantity of vegetables will stretch to stuff a second sea bass to feed up to 8.

Double the quantity of vegetables for three sea bass to feed 12 people, which should fit into the large roasting tin, covered with foil.

Serves 4

2 lb (1kg) whole sea bass

4 spring onions

2" piece root ginger

1 clove garlic

1 lime

1 tbsp white wine

1 tbsp grapeseed oil

1 tbsp sesame oil

3 tbsp soy sauce

1 tbsp chopped fresh coriander

Oven:

Roasting oven, 200C, 400F, Gas 6

Prepare in advance:

Prepare the fish and sauce, chill wrapped fish for 12 hours before baking

Prepare ahead:

Cooked, wrapped fish will keep warm for 1/2 hour in simmering oven. Pour over sauce just before serving

Freeze:

No

1   Gut and clean the fish then run a round bladed knife over the outside to remove the scales.

2   Trim the spring onions and cut into 2"/5cm lengths and shred into fine strips.

3   Peel the ginger and shred into fine strips. Peel and crush the garlic and grate the rind of the lime and squeeze the juice.

4   Make 3 slashes into each side of the fish and press a few of the spring onion and ginger strips into each cut and put some into the cavity of the fish. Pour over the lime juice and wine.

5   Wrap the fish in foil and lay onto a shallow baking tray. Hang the tray from the 4th runners in the roasting oven and bake for about 10–15 minutes, until the fish is almost cooked – it will continue to cook while you make the sauce.

6   Leave the fish wrapped while you make the sauce – heat the oils in a heavy based pan on the boiling plate and add the lime rind, garlic, the remaining spring onions and ginger. Stir fry for a minute or two, then add the soy sauce.

7   Unwrap the fish and set it onto a serving plate. Pour over the sauce, scatter over the coriander and serve at once.

prawn and
rocket risotto

To feed more people: Double the ingredients will feed 8, or up to 12 as a starter.

Serves 4

- 1 onion
- 1 clove garlic
- 2 tbsp olive oil
- 8 oz (½ pint in a measuring jug) (225g) risotto rice
- 2 tbsp sun dried tomato paste
- 1 pint (550ml) fish stock
- Salt and pepper
- 6 oz (175g) uncooked prawns
- Small bunch fresh rocket

Oven:

Aga simmering oven, 130C, 250F, Gas 1

Prepare ahead:

Will keep warm for up to an hour

Freeze:

Don't see why not!

1 Peel and chop the onion, crush the garlic. Heat the oil in a large pan and add onion, garlic and cook on the boiling plate for 2-3 minutes, then put on the floor of the roasting oven to continue cooking for a further 2-3 minutes to brown.

2 Stir in the rice, and pour over the stock. Season, stir well and bring to the boil on the boiling plate. Cover and put in the simmering oven for 20 minutes.

3 Once the rice has absorbed all of the stock, stir in the prawns. Re cover and return to the simmering oven for 5 minutes until the prawns are pink, then stir in the rocket and serve at once.

summer cod with oranges and tomatoes

This could be served hot with rice on a cool day or cold with salad on a hot day!

To feed more people: Double the ingredients will feed 8, three times the fish and double the sauce will feed 12.

Serves 4

4 cod loin steaks, about 6 oz (175g) each

1 tbsp Jamaican jerk seasoning

1 large orange

1 clove garlic

2 medium tomatoes

2 spring onions

Handful fresh basil leaves

4 tbsp olive oil

1 tsp balsamic vinegar

Oven:

Aga roasting oven, 200C, 400F, Gas 6

Prepare in advance:

Coat the fish and mix the dressing. Cook fish at the last minute before serving

Prepare ahead:

Keep the fish warm for up to half an hour in the simmering oven or set on top of the closed Aga lids to cool very slowly!

Freeze:

No, the sauce needs to be fresh

1   Wash and dry the fish steaks and set them on a plate. Pour over about a tablespoon of olive oil and smear or brush it over them, then sprinkle over half of the jerk seasoning. Turn the fish over and coat the other side with oil and seasoning.

2   Line the small shallow baking tray with Bake-O-Glide. Lay the fish pieces into the tray and hang it from the second set of runners in the roasting oven. Cook for about 8–12 minutes.

3   Peel and segment the orange – over a bowl to catch the juice! – and put the orange flesh into the bowl. Quarter and roughly chop the tomatoes and add them to the bowl.

4   Crush the garlic, trim and slice the spring onions and tear up the basil leaves and mix into the bowl of orange and tomato.

5   Pour on the remaining olive oil and balsamic vinegar and stir together.

6   Serve the fish steaks with the sauce poured over.

smoky fish pie

To feed more people: Double the quantity will make a fish pie to fill the large roasting tin and should give 10 portions.

Serves 4–5

1 lb potatoes

¼ pint (150ml) milk

1 oz butter

Salt and pepper

2 oz (55g) stilton cheese

1½ lb (600g) smoked haddock

1 tub (200g) crème fraîche

2 tbsp horseradish sauce

Salt and pepper

Oven:

Simmering oven, 250F, 130C, Gas 1 and roasting oven, 400F, 200C, Gas 6

Prepare in advance:

Keep in the fridge for up to 24 hours

Prepare ahead:

Keep warm in the simmering oven for an hour

Freeze:

Yes, defrost and reheat in roasting oven for half an hour

1 For the topping: Cut the potatoes into even sized pieces and put into a pan. Cover with water and bring to the boil. Once they have boiled for a minute, drain, cover and put into the simmering oven for 30 minutes until soft. Set the milk in a mug on the back of the Aga to warm up.

2 Mash the potatoes with the milk, cheese and butter, seasoning generously. Set aside to cool for a few minutes.

3 For the base of the pie: Cut the fish into 2"/5cm pieces and put into a wide ovenproof dish. Mix the crème fraîche with the horseradish and seasoning, then pour over the fish.

4 Pile to potato onto the fish and make pretty patterns with a fork (or pipe it on if you are feeling really keen).

5 Set the grid shelf on the third set of runners and put the pie onto the shelf and cook for 25 – 40 minutes until golden brown.

If there is any fish pie left over, mix together the remains and roll into balls to create fishcakes. Coat in seasoned flour then fry in a spoonful of olive oil in a pan on the floor of the roasting oven.

marinated monkfish kebabs

To feed more people: Double the quantity will give up to 10 portions – thread the skewers with fewer chunks of fish to make it stretch! Grill in the large shallow baking tray.

Serves 4

1 lb (450g) monkfish tail

2 onions

2 red peppers

1 tbsp Thai fish sauce

1 tbsp sesame oil

2 Thai lime leaves

1 clove garlic, crushed

Salt and pepper

Oven:

Very top of roasting oven or a grill or barbecue

Prepare in advance:

Kebabs will keep, uncooked, in the fridge for up to 24 hours

Prepare ahead:

Will keep warm in simmering oven for half an hour

Freeze:

Yes, uncooked

1   Soak some wooden skewers in water.

2   Cut the fish into 1½"/3cm chunks. Peel and quarter the onion and cut the pepper into 2"/5cm chunks.

3   Thread the fish, onion and pepper onto the skewers, alternating each.

4   Mix together the oil, fish sauce, garlic and seasoning – you could add an optional chopped red chilli if you like – and crumble in the lime leaf. Pour this marinade over the fish skewers and lay on a shallow Portmerion Aga dish, cover and refrigerate for a couple of hours for the flavours to mingle.

5   When you are ready to cook the kebabs, baste with the marinade then hang the dish from the top set of runners in the roasting oven for 10 minutes. Remove from the oven, turn the skewers over and return to the oven for a further 5 minutes to finish cooking. Serve at once, scattered with chopped coriander.

thai fish curry

To feed more people: Double the ingredients will feed 8 or 9 with lots of rice, more if served as part of a Thai buffet.

Serves 4

4 cod loin steaks

2 tbsp groundnut oil

1 bunch spring onions

1 clove garlic

1 tin (400ml) coconut milk

4 Thai lime leaves

2 tbsp fish sauce

1 tbsp Thai red curry paste

¼ pint (150ml) stock

1 tbsp chopped fresh coriander

Oven:

Floor of roasting oven, 200C, 400F, Gas 6 and simmering oven, 130C, 250F, Gas 1

Prepare in advance:

Chop ingredients and cook sauce up to 24 hours in advance, but do not cook fish until just before serving

Prepare ahead:

Will keep warm in simmering oven for an hour

Freeze:

Yes

1 Peel and crush the garlic; trim and slice the spring onions. Cut the fish into 1" cubes.

2 Heat the oil in a deep frying pan or casserole. Add the onions, garlic and all the remaining ingredients except the fish to the pan, stir together and bring to the boil, then add the fish, cover and put into the simmering oven for 5–10 minutes until cooked through.

3 Serve the fish on top of some rice, with the sauce poured over and a scattering of chopped fresh coriander leaves.

cumin chicken salad

To feed more people: Double the quantity will feed up to 10 people, more if it is served as a starter.

Serves 4

4 skinless chicken breast fillets

2 tbsp olive oil

1 tsp ground cumin

½ tsp chilli powder

1 small red onion

4 oz (110g) broad beans

8 oz (225g) cherry tomatoes

1 round lettuce

2 avocado pears

Dressing:

3 tbsp olive oil

1 tbsp balsamic vinegar

½ tsp brown sugar

Salt and pepper

Oven:

Aga roasting oven, 200C, 400F, Gas 6

Prepare in advance:

Salad will keep in fridge for 24 hours, do not dress until ready to eat

Prepare ahead:

Cook chicken and keep warm in simmering oven and add to salad before dressing it.

Freeze:

No, except the beans!

1   Cut the chicken into 1" chunks. Mix the oil and spices in a bowl and add the chicken pieces. Stir together, cover and leave to marinate for an hour if possible (or overnight).

2   Line a shallow baking tin with Bake-O-Glide and put the chicken into the tin. Hang from the second runners in the roasting oven and cook for about 15 minutes until cooked but not crisp.

3   Meanwhile, put the broad beans into a pan and cover with cold water. Set on the boiling plate and bring to the boil. Once boiling hard, drain and tip the beans into a bowl of cold water – this will help keep them green as they cool.

4   Wash the lettuce and tear the leaves into smallish pieces. Halve the tomatoes, peel and chop the onion. Quarter, peel and roughly chop the avocados.

5   Put all the vegetables into a large bowl. Mix the dressing ingredients together – shaken in a jam jar is simplest.

6   Take the chicken from the oven and tip it onto the salad. Toss in the dressing and serve at once.

lazy sunday chicken

To feed more people: A bigger chicken will feed more people – a 4lb bird will feed up to 7, especially if you are generous with doubling the quantity of vegetables! Two 3lb chickens with double all the other ingredients will feed 8 – 10, easily.

Serves 4

3 lb (1.5 kg) chicken

2 oz (55g) butter

2 lemons

2 cloves garlic

2 onions

1 lb (450g) carrots

1 lb (450g) new potatoes

2 sticks celery

Gravy:

1 tbsp plain flour

1 pint (500ml) chicken stock

Salt and pepper

Oven:

Simmering oven, 130C, 250F, Gas 1, then roasting oven, 200C, 400F, Gas 6

Prepare in advance:

Cooked cooled chicken and vegetables will keep in the fridge for up to 24 hours

Prepare ahead:

Will keep warm in simmering oven for an extra hour

Freeze:

Not really, the vegetables go a bit soggy as they defrost

1   Set the butter in a bowl on the back of the Aga to melt, while you prepare the vegetables.

2   Peel and chop the onion, crush the garlic. Cut the carrots into 2"/5cms lengths and cut the celery into 1"/2.5 cms lengths.

3   Add the crushed garlic to the bowl of butter. Grate in the lemon rind and squeeze in the juice. Mix together – and smear this lemon paste all over the chicken. Put the empty lemon halves into the chicken cavities.

4   Line the small roasting tin with Bake-O-Glide and tip in all the prepared vegetables, then put the chicken on top, so that it is sitting in a jumble of vegetables. Cover the tin with foil and put into the simmering oven. Cook for at least 3 hours, up to 4 hours.

5   When the chicken is cooked, remove from the simmering oven, uncover and scoop all the vegetables out of the tin into a serving dish. Transfer the uncovered chicken to the roasting oven for 10 minutes to brown.

6   Once the chicken has browned, remove from the oven and transfer to a plate to rest while you make the gravy: Stir the flour into the chicken juices in the roasting tin, then add the stock, stirring all the time. Season well. Put the tin onto the floor of the roasting oven for 5 minutes until the gravy is boiling.

7   Carve the chicken and serve it with the vegetables and gravy.

tarragon chicken

To feed more people: Allow one breast or two thighs per person. Double the marinade will flavour up to 10 servings.

Serves 4

4 chicken breasts or 8 chicken thighs

Handful fresh tarragon

1 clove garlic

6 spring onions

1 tbsp olive oil

2 tbsp red wine vinegar

Pinch sugar

Salt and pepper

2 tbsp natural yogurt

Oven:

Roasting oven, 200C, 400F, Gas 6

Prepare in advance:

Meat will keep in its marinade in the bag for up to 24 hours in fridge

Prepare ahead:

Keep warm for up to half an hour in the simmering oven

Freeze:

Yes, uncooked chicken in its bag

1 Put the chicken meat into a sturdy plastic bag.

2 Peel and crush the garlic, trim and slice the spring onions and chop the tarragon.

3 Tip the garlic, onions, tarragon, oil, vinegar and seasoning into the bag with the chicken, seal and shake to coat the meat in the marinade. Leave to marinate for at least an hour, preferably longer.

4 Line the small roasting tin with Bake-O-Glide and pour in the chicken and its marinade.

5 Hang the tin from the third runners in the roasting oven and bake for about 20 minutes until the chicken is cooked. Remove the meat from the tin to rest while you finish the sauce.

6 Stir the yogurt in the juices in the tin and set the tin onto the floor of the roasting oven for a couple of minutes to boil and reduce a little.

7 Serve the chicken with the sauce poured over and a little more chopped tarragon scattered over the top.

stir-fried
chicken satay

To feed more people: Double the ingredients will feed up to 10.

Serves 4

6 boneless chicken thigh joints

1 red chilli

1"/2 cm piece ginger

1 clove garlic

2 tbsp crunchy peanut butter

2 tbsp chopped fresh coriander

1 tsp caster sugar

4 spring onions

2 tbsp rice vinegar

3 tbsp groundnut oil

1 tbsp Thai fish sauce (nam pla)

Oven:

Boiling plate

Prepare in advance:

24 hours in the marinade

Prepare ahead:

Keep warm for up to 30 minutes in the warming oven

Freeze:

Yes, uncooked in the marinade

1   Cut the chicken meat into thin strips and put into a heavy duty plastic bag.

2   Halve the chilli, remove the seeds and the white membrane (this is the hottest part!) and chop finely with the peeled garlic and ginger. Add the rice vinegar, coriander, sugar, oil, trimmed spring onions, peanut butter and fish sauce and mix. Tip into the plastic bag and seal, then shake to coat the meat in the marinade.

3   Leave to marinate for at least an hour, or overnight if possible.

4   Put a wok or deep, heavy frying pan into the roasting oven to heat up – cast iron takes up to 10 minutes, cast aluminium about 5 minutes.

5   Transfer the hot pan to the boiling plate and tip in the contents of the bag.

6   Stir-fry for about 10 minutes, then serve on a bed of rice.

singapore stir-fried noodles

To feed more people: Double the quantity will give 10 portions, or 12 if served as part of a larger buffet

Serves 4 – 5

2 tbsp sunflower oil

½"/1cm root ginger

1 red chilli

1 clove garlic

1 tsp turmeric

10 oz (300g) fine rice noodles

4 oz (110g) shiitake mushrooms

6 oz (175g) raw peeled king prawns

1 red pepper

1 carrot

3 tbsp bean sprouts

3 spring onions

4 oz (110g) cooked chicken

2 tbsp soy sauce

2 tbsp oyster sauce

1 tbsp rice vinegar

1 tsp sesame oil

1 egg

Oven:

Boiling plate

Prepare in advance:

Chop and mix all the ingredients and keep refrigerated until ready to stir fry

Prepare ahead:

No, eat this as soon as it is cooked

Freeze:

No

1   Peel and trim the ginger, chilli and garlic, then chop them together, with the turmeric.

2   Put a heavy based pan or wok into the roasting oven to heat up.

3   Put the noodles into a pan and pour over a kettle of boiling water. Leave to stand for 5 minutes while you chop the rest of the ingredients, then drain.

4   Trim and thinly slice the mushrooms, pepper, spring onions and carrot. Shred the chicken meat. Mix together the soy sauce, oyster sauce, rice vinegar and sesame oil in a jam jar.

5   Heat the sunflower oil in the pan, then add the ginger, garlic and chilli mixture and stir fry for a minute. Add the prawns and stir fry for a minute or two until beginning to turn pink, then add the chicken and the vegetables and toss in the pan over the heat, stir frying until well mixed.

6   Tip the noodles into the pan, and stir over the heat, then add the soy sauce mixture.

7   Beat the egg and stir in, then serve at once as the egg begins to set.

For a more robust and fiery stir fry, add some dried chilli flakes or more red chillis.

sesame chicken stir fry

To feed more people: Double the quantity will give 10 portions.

Serves 4–5

4 chicken breast fillets

1 tbsp groundnut oil

1 tbsp sesame oil

1 tbsp white vermouth

1 tbsp soy sauce

6 spring onions

1 clove garlic

6 oz (175g) mushrooms

2 tbsp sesame seeds

1 tbsp pine nuts

1 bunch watercress

Salt and pepper

Oven:

Boiling plate

Prepare in advance:

Put the meat in the marinade and keep in the fridge for up to 24 hours but do not cook until the last minute

Prepare ahead:

Keep warm in the simmering or warming oven for 10 minutes

Freeze:

Not this one, the mushrooms spoil in the freezer.

1   Cut the chicken into ½"/1cm slices. Trim and chop the spring onions. Crush the garlic. Wipe and quarter the mushrooms. Put everything into a bowl with the oil, vermouth and soy sauce and stir to mix. Leave to marinate for at least an hour.

2   Put a heavy pan into the roasting oven for 5 minutes to heat up. Toast the sesame seeds and pine nuts in the pan on the boiling plate for a minute or two, then set aside.

3   Tip the chicken mixture into the hot pan and stir fry for 5–8 minutes, until the chicken is just cooked. Remove from the heat and stir in the watercress, sesame seeds and pine nuts.

4   Serve at once, with Aga rice.

For any stir fry in the Aga, put the pan or wok into the Roasting oven to heat up whilst you chop the ingredients, so that the pan is really hot and ready to cook when you are. If you are stir frying with a bag of bought ingredients, put the pan into the oven, have a glass of wine and do a moderate sudoku puzzle, which takes just about long enough to heat the pan!

chiang mai chicken curry

Serves 4

1 lb (450g) chicken breasts

1 tin (340g) coconut milk

3 tbsp Thai green curry paste

1 medium aubergine

1 tsp soft brown sugar

2 tbsp Thai fish sauce

3 Thai lime leaves, crushed

2 tbsp basil leaves

1 green chilli

1 bunch spring onions

Oven:

Simmering oven, 130C, 250F, Gas 1

Prepare in advance:

Keep in the fridge for up to 24 hours

Prepare ahead:

Will keep warm in the simmering oven for half an hour

Freeze:

Yes, reheat in the roasting oven for 25 minutes, but use chicken thighs instead of breasts, which tend to go a little stringy when re-heated after freezing

1 Cut the chicken into thin slices. Trim and slice the spring onions, crush the garlic, chop the chilli and cut the aubergine into $1/2$" (1cm) chunks.

2 Heat a heavy based pan in the roasting oven, then transfer to the boiling plate and add the meat, onions, garlic and aubergine. Stir fry for a couple of minutes, then stir in the rest of the ingredients, reserving half of the basil leaves to scatter over the finished dish.

3 Bring to the boil then cover and transfer to the simmering oven for 10 minutes. Serve with Aga rice.

springtime chicken

This seems like a lot of juggling between ovens, but it is worth it for this one-pot supper!

To feed more people: Double the ingredients should give up to 10 portions.

Serves 4

4 chicken breasts

1 tbsp olive oil

12 oz (675g) small new potatoes, washed

1 pint (550ml) chicken stock

1 lb (450g) selection of spring vegetables – whatever you have to hand, including broad beans, peas, sugar snaps, mangetout, French beans, courgettes and broccoli

3 tbsp crème fraîche

Sprig fresh tarragon, chopped

Salt and pepper

Oven:

Floor of roasting oven, simmering oven, 130C, 250F, Gas

Prepare in advance:

Cooked and chilled, refrigerate for 24 hours

Prepare ahead:

Keep warm in simmering oven for half an hour

Freeze:

Yes, defrost and reheat in roasting oven for 30 minutes. If freezing, use chicken thighs as they are more forgiving than breasts, which tend to go a little stringy when reheated from the freezer.

1 Heat the oil in a wide deep sauté pan on the simmering plate. Add the chicken, skin side down, then transfer to the floor of the roasting oven for 5–7 minutes to brown.

2 Slice the potatoes and add to the pan, with the stock. Season and bring to the boil, then cover and transfer to the simmering oven for 20 minutes.

3 Return to the boiling plate, remove the lid and add the vegetables – you might want to cut up the broccoli and halve the French beans. Return the pan to the floor of the roasting oven, without a lid, and boil hard for 5 minutes until the vegetables are tender and the sauce reduced.

4 Stir in the crème fraîche, seasoning and tarragon. Serve at once.

chinese chicken legs

To feed more people: Allow one whole chicken leg per person. Double the other ingredients will make enough sauce for 12 chicken legs.

Serves 4

4 chicken legs, thigh and drumstick attached

2 tbsp sunflower oil

4 tbsp runny honey

2 cloves garlic

1 tsp Chinese five-spice powder

1"/2cm root ginger

¼ pint (150ml) stock

5 tbsp soy sauce

1 bunch spring onions

2 red chillies

Oven:

Roasting oven, 200C, 400F, Gas 6

Prepare in advance:

Mix the chicken with the cooled marinade and refrigerate for 24 hours

Prepare ahead:

Keep warm in simmering oven for half an hour

Freeze:

Yes, either before or after cooking

1   Crush the garlic, finely chop the chillies and ginger. Slice the spring onions.

2   Heat the oil in a deep sauté pan on the simmering plate and add the garlic, chillies and ginger until sizzling. Add the stock and soy sauce. Cover and put into the simmering oven for 5 minutes then remove from the oven and allow to cool if time permits.

3   Line the small roasting tin with Bake-O-Glide and put the chicken into it. Mix together the honey and five-spice powder and rub into the meat. Pour over the sauce and cover with foil.

4   Hang the tin from the 4th runners in the roasting oven for about 20 minutes, then remove the foil and continue to cook for a further 15 minutes.

5   Serve the chicken legs on a bed of rice, with the sauce poured over and the spring onions scattered on top.

tandoori chicken

Serves 4

12 chicken leg pieces

1 tsp salt

1 lemon

½ pint (300ml) yogurt

1 onion

1 clove garlic

½" (2cm) piece fresh ginger

1 green chilli

2 tsp garam masala

1. Cut deep slits in the chicken meat, all the way to the bone.

2. Put the chicken into a large, serious plastic bag, with the grated rind and juice of the lemon. Seal the bag and allow to stand for half an hour.

3. Peel the onion and garlic. Put them into a processor, with the chilli, garam masala and yogurt. Whizz. Tip into the bag of chicken and lemon, re-seal the bag and leave to marinate for at least 6 hours, preferably overnight.

tandoori chicken *continued*

Oven:

Roasting oven, 425F, 220C, Gas 7

Prepare in advance:

Leave chicken in marinade for up to 2 days

Prepare ahead:

Keep cooked chicken warm in simmering oven for an hour

4   Tip the contents of the bag into a shallow baking tray, lined with Bake-O-Glide. Shake to spread them out evenly, then hang the tin on the 2nd runners and bake for 20–25 minutes. Serve with lemon wedges.

Freeze:

Yes, either in marinade or cooked

thai chicken curry

If you prefer a hotter curry, add a chopped red chilli or two …

To feed more people: Double the ingredients will feed 8 or 9, more if served as part of a Thai buffet.

Serves 4

1lb (450g) chicken breast fillet

1 tbsp groundnut oil

4 spring onions

1 clove garlic

3 Thai lime leaves

3 tbsp Thai red curry paste

1/2 tsp caster sugar

2 tbsp Thai fish sauce (nam pla)

1/2 can (200ml) coconut milk

1/4 pint (150ml) stock

2 medium courgettes

4 oz (110g) cherry tomatoes

Handful coriander leaves

Oven:

Aga roasting oven, 400F, 200C, Gas 6, then simmering oven

Prepare ahead:

Will keep in fridge for 24 hours

1   Put a large heavy, ovenproof, frying pan into the roasting oven to heat up.

2   Cut the chicken into 1"/5cm chunks. Trim and slice the spring onions. Crush the garlic. Cut the courgettes into 1/2" dice and halve the tomatoes.

3   Heat the oil in the pan on the boiling plate and tip in the chicken and set it on the floor of the roasting oven to fry for a few minutes. Stir once.

4   When browned, remove from the oven to the simmering plate and stir in the lime leaves and curry paste. Add the sugar, courgettes, the garlic, spring onions and fish sauce, then the coconut milk and stock and stir until it boils. Cover and put into the simmering oven for 10 minutes.

5   Put the pan back onto the simmering plate and add the tomatoes, stir then serve, scattered with chopped coriander.

Freeze:

Yes

spanish rice

To feed more people: Double the ingredients will feed 8 people, maybe 10 if served with other side dishes.

Serves 4

8 oz (half a pint in a measuring jug) (225g) long grain rice

1 medium onion

2 cloves garlic

2 tbsp olive oil

½ pint (300ml) chicken stock

1 tin (340g) chopped tomatoes

1 lb (450g) chicken meat

8 oz (225g) chorizo sausage

1 tsp smoked paprika

Salt and pepper

Parsley to garnish

Oven:

Aga simmering oven, 130C, 250F, Gas 1

Prepare in advance:

Cooked, cooled rice will keep in fridge for 24 hours

Prepare ahead:

Will keep warm for an hour in the simmering oven

Freeze:

Yes, defrost and reheat in roasting oven for half an hour

1   Peel and chop the onion, crush the garlic. Cut the chicken into 2"/5cms chunks and the chorizo into 1"/2½cms chunks.

2   Heat the oil in a heavy pan on the simmering plate, and add the chicken, onion and garlic. When sizzling, transfer to the floor of the roasting oven for 10 minutes, shaking the pan occasionally to brown the meat evenly.

3   Transfer the pan to the simmering plate and stir in the rice, tomatoes, paprika, seasoning and chorizo. Bring to the boil, then cover and put into the simmering oven for at least 15 minutes.

4   Serve with a scattering of chopped parsley.

chicken and leek pie

To feed more people: Double the quantity will feed up to 10; cook it in the large roasting tin.

Serves 4

1 oz (25g) butter

4 leeks

1 clove garlic

4 chicken breast fillets

1 tbsp plain flour

1 tsp chicken stock powder

½ pint (300ml) milk

Salt and pepper

1 packet (375g) ready-rolled puff pastry

1 egg

Oven:

Simmering oven 130C, 250F, Gas 1 and Roasting oven 200C, 400F, Gas 6

Prepare in advance:

Uncooked, assembled pie will keep in the fridge for up to 24 hours

Prepare ahead:

Keep warm in simmering oven for half an hour

Freeze:

Uncooked, assembled pie

1   Trim and slice the leeks, crush the garlic and cut the chicken meat into 1"/2cms chunks.

2   Melt the butter in a pan on the boiling plate and stir in the leeks, garlic and chicken. Once the pan is sizzling, cover and put into the simmering oven for 15–20 minutes to cook the chicken and soften the leeks.

3   Transfer the pan to the simmering plate and stir in the flour. When well blended, add the stock powder and milk, stirring all the time and bring to the boil. Season and tip into a pie dish to cool.

4   Unroll the pastry and lay it over the top of the chicken mixture, decorating with some trimmings if you are feeling keen. Brush with beaten egg.

5   Set the grid shelf on the floor of the roasting oven and set the pie onto it. Bake for about 20 minutes until the pastry is puffy and golden and the filling is bubbling.

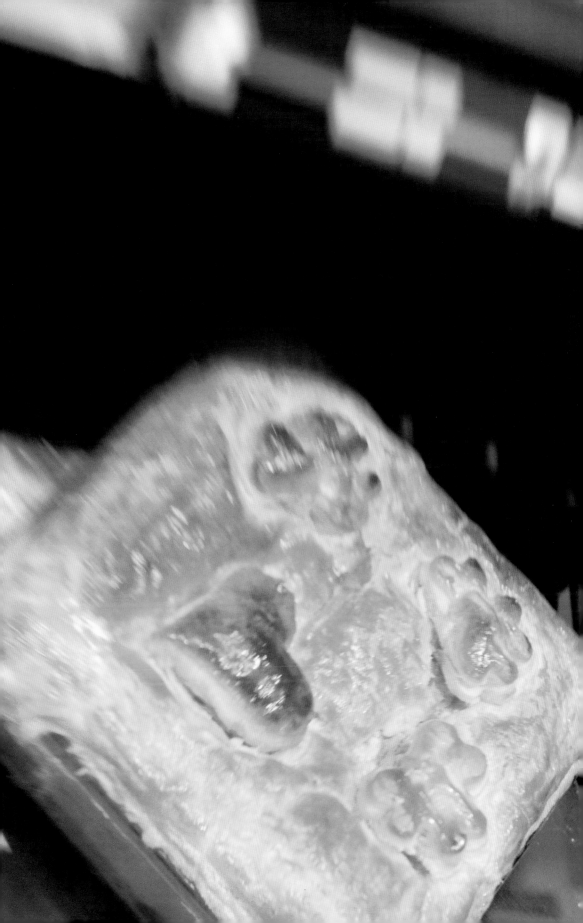

sticky chicken

To feed more people: Cut the breasts into 1"/2cm slices to serve 5. Double the ingredients, also sliced, will feed up to 10. Three times the amount of chicken will only need double the sauce ingredients.

Serves 4

4 chicken breasts

3 tbsp sweet chilli sauce

½"/1cm fresh ginger

1 clove garlic

2 tsp soy sauce

1 lemon

2 tbsp chopped fresh coriander to serve

Oven:

Roasting oven, 200C, 400F, Gas 6

Prepare in advance:

Uncooked chicken will sit in its marinade in the fridge for up to 48 hours

Prepare ahead:

Keep warm in simmering oven for up to an hour

Freeze:

Uncooked chicken in marinade

1   Cut the chicken meat into 1" / 2cms chunks.

2   Grate the lemon rind, garlic and ginger into a large plastic bag.

3   Add the chilli and soy sauces and the juice of the lemon to the bag.

4   Add the chicken to the bag and seal it tightly. Roll it about to coat the meat in the marinade and leave to absorb the flavours for at least an hour, if not overnight in the fridge.

5   Line the shallow baking tray with Bake-O-Glide and tip the chicken into it.

6   Hang the tin from the 2nd runners in the roasting oven and bake until golden and even stickier – about 20 minutes.

7   Serve with the coriander scattered over the top. Served with rice or spiced mashed potatoes.

If you are going to freeze the chicken after it has been cooked, use chicken thigh or leg joints, these are much more forgiving to reheat once cooked, as chicken breasts tend to go a bit stringy.

chicken korma

To feed more people: Double all the ingredients will feed 12 people. Double the other ingredients, but triple the meat, will feed 18 people; cook in the simmering oven for at least 40 minutes.

As part of a large meal, with other curries, allow half a portion per person.

Serves 6

6 chicken breasts

1 onion

2 cloves garlic

2 tbsp vegetable oil

2 tomatoes

1 green chilli

1 tsp chilli powder

½ tsp ground turmeric

2 tbsp yogurt

1 can coconut milk

1 tsp cloves

1 tsp cardamom seeds

1 tsp ground ginger

1 stick cinnamon

1 tsp chopped fresh mint

2 tbsp chopped fresh coriander

Oven:

Simmering oven, 130C, 250F, Gas 1

Prepare in advance:

Cooked, cooled korma will keep in fridge for 24 hours

Prepare ahead:

Will keep warm in simmering oven for an extra hour

Freeze:

Yes

1   Peel and slice the onions, peel and crush the garlic.

2   Heat the oil in a heavy casserole and add the chicken meat, garlic and onions. Transfer to the floor of the roasting oven to brown for 5 minutes, then shake and return to the oven for a further 5 minutes.

3   Chop the tomatoes and chilli and add to the pan, with the ginger and ground spices and fry again for few minutes.

4   Add the yogurt, coconut milk, chopped coriander, mint and salt and bring to the boil.

5   Cover and put into the simmering oven for 25 minutes.

pheasant cream

To feed more people: Allow 1 pheasant breast per person, but double the quantity of sauce will cover 10 portions.

You could also use a whole, roasted or poached(!) pheasant for this, one bird and one quantity of sauce will serve about 3 people.

Serves 4

4 pheasant breasts

1 pint (550ml) water

1 bay leaf

½ onion

½ pint (300ml) double cream

4 tbsp Worcester sauce

4 tbsp mango chutney

Salt and pepper

Oven:

Roasting oven, 400F, 200C, Gas 6

Prepare in advance:

Assemble the dish and keep refrigerated for up to 24 hours

Prepare ahead:

Keep warm in the simmering oven for half an hour

Freeze:

No

1 Peel and roughly chop the onion. Put the water, bayleaf and onion into a pan and add the pheasant breasts. Set on the boiling plate and bring to the boil. Cover and put into the simmering oven for about 15 minutes to poach the pheasant.

2 When the pheasant is cooked, remove from the pan and slice neatly. Lay the slices in a wide, shallow serving dish, cover and set in the simmering oven to keep warm.

3 Strain the poaching stock – keep it for another day!

4 Pour about 2 tbsp of the stock into the warm pan, add the cream, chutney and Worcester sauce. Season well and heat on the simmering plate until almost boiling, stirring occasionally.

5 Pour the sauce over the pheasant and serve with rice or mashed potatoes.

rabbit and mustard casserole

Serves 4

1 lb (450g) diced rabbit

2 tbsp olive oil

1 medium onion

1 clove garlic

2 tbsp grainy mustard

1 tbsp plain flour

¼ pint (150ml) stock

Handful fresh parsley, chopped

Oven:

Floor of roasting oven, then simmering oven, 130C, 250F, Gas 1

Prepare in advance:

Cooked, cooled casserole will keep in the fridge for 24 hours

Prepare ahead:

Will keep warm in simmering oven for an extra hour or so

Freeze:

Yes

1   Cut the meat into ½"/1cm cubes. Peel and slice the onion and crush the garlic.

2   Heat the oil in a heavy pan and add the meat, garlic and onions. Stir over the heat until sizzling, then transfer to the floor of the roasting oven for 10 minutes to brown, shaking once or twice to turn the meat.

3   Tip in the mustard, flour and stock, stirring well to blend. Bring to the boil, then cover and put into the simmering oven for 45 minutes.

4   Stir in the crème fraîche, scatter over the parsley and serve with rice or couscous.

duck stir fry
for clementine

To feed more people: Four duck breasts with the same amount of other ingredients will feed 6, double all the ingredients will feed 8 to 10, especially if served with lots of rice!

Serves 4

2 (large!) duck breast fillets

2 heads pak choi

4 oz (110g) bean sprouts

8 oz (225g) medium egg noodles

2 cloves garlic

1"/2cms piece root ginger

1 red chilli

6 spring onions

2 tbsp groundnut or rapeseed oil

Sauce:

1 tbsp sun dried tomato purée

1 tbsp sesame oil

1 tbsp soy sauce

1 tbsp rice vinegar

Oven:

Boiling plate

Prepare in advance:

Prepare all the meat and vegetables, then stir fry just before serving

Prepare ahead:

Doesn't really keep warm well, the vegetables and noodles go soggy

Freeze:

No, see above

1 Put a heavy sauté pan or wok into the roasting oven to heat up.

2 Remove the skins from the duck breasts and slice thinly.

3 Slice the pak choi. Peel the garlic and ginger and chop together very finely, with the chilli. Trim and slice the spring onions.

4 Mix the sauce ingredients together – easiest in a jam jar, just put on the lid and shake!

5 Cook the noodles according to the packet instructions, drain and return to their cooking pan to keep warm.

6 Transfer the hot pan to the boiling plate and add the oil, then the duck meat. Stir fry for a couple of minutes, then add the chilli, garlic, ginger and spring onions. Stir fry for a minute, then tip the noodles, pak choi and bean sprouts into the pan.

7 Continue to stir fry for another minute, until the pak choi is beginning to wilt, then pour in the sauce, mix well and serve at once.

spiced orange duck

To serve more people: Remove the cooked meat from the bones and share it around 6 plates. Double the ingredients, with the cooked meat off the bones, should feed 10 to 12.

Serves 4

4 duck legs

1 large onion

1 clove garlic

1 tbsp olive oil

1 tsp ground cumin

1 tsp ground ginger

1 tsp ground coriander

1 tsp smoked paprika

1 tsp runny honey

2 oranges

3/4 pint (425ml) stock

2 tbsp fresh coriander to finish

Oven:

Aga roasting oven 200C, 400F, Gas 6 then simmering oven 130C, 250F, Gas 1

Prepare in advance:

The duck improves after 24 hours in a fridge!

Prepare ahead:

Keep in simmering oven for an additional hour or two

Freeze: *Yes*

Freeze the duck fat in small batches for roast potatoes and fried bread in the future!

1   Line the large roasting tin with Bake-O-Glide and set the grill rack into it.

2   Put the duck legs onto the grill rack and hang the tin from the third runners in the roasting oven for about 45 minutes until golden.

3   Peel and chop the onion and crush the garlic. Wash and slice the oranges.

4   Heat the oil in a large heavy pan on the simmering plate and add the onion and garlic. When sizzling, cover and transfer to the simmering oven for 15 minutes or so, to soften.

5   Take the onions from the oven and transfer to the simmering plate. Add the spices and sliced oranges, honey and stock. Bring to the boil, then add the browned duck legs.

6   Cover and put in the simmering oven for at least an hour, but up to 2 hours.

7   Scatter some chopped coriander over the duck and serve with couscous.

Ring the changes:

• Try using a couple of rounds of stem ginger (grated) instead of the orange. Leave out the coriander, substituting parsley.

partridge pie

To feed more people: Double the quantity will make one very large pie (use the Aga buffet pan) or two smaller ones and should feed up to 10, especially if served with lots of potatoes!

Serves 4

8 partridge breasts or 4 partridge

1 onion

1 clove garlic

1 oz (25g) butter

1 tbsp olive oil

1 tbsp plain flour

1/2 pint (300ml) stock

1 tsp juniper berries

1 tbsp cranberry sauce

Salt and pepper

1 pack (375g) ready-rolled puff pastry

1 egg

Oven:

Roasting oven, 200C, 400F, Gas 6 and simmering oven, 130C, 250F, Gas 1

Prepare in advance:

Prepared, unbaked pie will keep in the fridge for 24 hours before baking

Prepare ahead:

Cooked pie will keep warm in simmering oven for an hour

Freeze:

Yes, unbaked pie

1   Slice the partridge breasts or remove all the flesh from the whole partridges and cut into slices or chunks.

2   Peel and chop the onion, crush the garlic.

3   Heat the oil and butter in a heavy pan and add the partridge meat, onion and garlic. Stir over the heat until sizzling then transfer to the floor of the roasting oven for about 5 minutes to brown.

4   Move the pan to the simmering plate and stir in the flour, then the stock, juniper berries and cranberry sauce. Bring to the boil, stirring all the time, season well then cover and transfer to the simmering oven for about 20 minutes until the meat is tender.

5   Remove from the oven and allow to cool completely. (You could serve it as a casserole at this point.)

6   Open out the pastry and lay it over the pan of cold meat. Trim to fit and cut any trimmings into pretty shapes to decorate the top of the pie. Brush with beaten egg.

7   Set the pie onto the floor of the roasting oven and bake for about 20 minutes until it is bubbling and the pastry is puffed up and golden.

Alternatives:

• Try using pheasant instead of some or all of the partridge

• Stretch one or two partridges by adding the same quantity of chicken or rabbit thigh meat

• Any stew or casserole can be turned into a pie by covering it with pastry and baking it!

beef wellington

To feed more people: Cut the beef into thinner slices! A second fillet in the same pastry case will feed up to 16, but a second Wellington in its own pastry case will feed up to 24.

Serves 8 – 10

Whole fillet of beef (about 3lbs, 1.6kg)

2 tbsp olive oil

2 cloves garlic

2 packs (2 x 375g) ready rolled puff pastry

1 pack (200g) smooth pâté – mushroom or liver is nice!

Oven:

Roasting oven, 200C, 400F, Gas 6

Prepare in advance:

Uncooked pastry parcel will keep in the fridge for 24 hours

Prepare ahead:

Will keep warm for up to an hour

Freeze:

Yes, uncooked pastry parcel

Whether serving hot, tepid or cold, it is important to eat the Wellington on the day that it has been cooked, if at all possible, as the pastry really does not do justice to the meat once it has been cooked and refrigerated.

1 Smear the oil over the meat and crush the garlic and rub it over the oily meat. Grind on some salt and pepper then put into the large roasting tin, lined with Bake-O-Glide and hang from the 2nd runners in the roasting oven for 20 minutes.

2 Once the meat is browned, remove from the oven and allow to cool completely. Reserve the juices in the roasting tin for the gravy.

3 Lay a sheet of Bake-O-Glide on the plain shelf. Unroll a sheet of puff pastry onto it. Brush the edges with beaten egg. Lay the cold meat onto the pastry.

4 Spread the pâté over the meat. Fold the edges of the pastry around the meat.

5 Brush the newly exposed pastry with beaten egg. Unroll the second sheet of pastry and lay it over the meat parcel, tucking the edges together. Brush with beaten egg to glaze. Make pretty shapes (leaves, letters, etc) with any pastry trimmings and decorate the Wellington, then glaze the decorations with more egg.

6 Set the plain shelf onto the floor of the roasting oven and bake for about 20 minutes until puffed up and golden.

serious stew
with dumplings!

If your guests are averse to dumplings, make one big, flat dumpling and cook it whole on the top of the stew, then call it a cobbler!

To feed more people: Double the ingredients should feed up to 14.

Serves 6

2½ lb (1½ kg) stewing beef

2 tbsp olive oil

2 medium onions

2 cloves garlic

2 tbsp plain flour

1 tsp fresh thyme leaves

Salt and pepper

1 tbsp Worcestershire sauce

1 tbsp sun dried tomato purée

1 pint (550ml) best bitter

Dumplings:

2 oz (55g) butter

4 oz (110g) self raising flour

2 tbsp horseradish cream

Salt and pepper

About 2 tbsp cold water (maybe a little more, maybe a little less!)

Oven:

Floor of roasting oven and simmering oven, 130C, 250F, Gas 1

Prepare in advance:

Cooked, cooled stew improves in the fridge for up to 48 hours

Prepare ahead:

Keep warm for an extra hour in the simmering oven

Freeze:

Yes, but not the dumplings!

1 Trim the beef and cut it into 1"/2cm cubes. Peel and chop the onion, crush the garlic.

2 Heat a heavy casserole on the boiling plate and add the meat and vegetables. Stir to coat everything in the hot oil and transfer to the floor of the roasting oven for 5 minutes to brown. Shake the pan to turn the meat and return to the floor of the oven for a further 5 minutes.

3 Move the pan to the simmering plate and stir in the flour, thyme, seasoning, Worcestershire sauce and tomato purée. Stir to blend everything together, then add the beer.

4 Bring the pan to the boil, stirring occasionally, then cover and transfer to the simmering oven for about 2 hours until the meat is tender.

5 For the dumplings: Either grate the chilled butter into a bowl and add the flour and horseradish, or tip everything in to a processor and whizz until it is blended. Add water a teaspoon at a time until you have a soft dough. Form into about a dozen balls with your hands.

6 Take the stew from the oven, remove the lid and add the dumplings. Return the casserole, uncovered, to the oven for a further half hour until the dumplings are puffed up and golden.

stew variations

1 You could add any or all of:

- a generous spoonful of horseradish sauce
- a spoonful of quince or redcurrant jelly
- a couple of sliced carrots
- a couple of sticks of celery
- a sliced leek

to the stew at the same time as the flour, flavourings and liquid.

2 You could add any one of:

- 4–6oz (120–175g) quartered mushrooms
- or a packet of peeled, prepared chestnuts
- or a tin of smoked oysters

to the stew at the same time as the dumplings.

3 You could substitute:

- Red or white wine instead of the beer
- Stock instead of the beer
- Stout instead of the bitter

4 You could substitute more chopped fresh thyme to the dumplings instead of the horseradish.

5 You could leave out the dumplings altogether, but they are a good teenage-boy filler!

fillet steaks with rich mushroom sauce

To feed more people: Double the quantity will feed 4, triple the quantity of meat but double the sauce will feed 6. If you are contemplating serving fillet steaks to more than 6, just double the quantity for every two people.

Serves 2

2 fillet steaks

1 tbsp butter

4 oz mushrooms, sliced

1 clove garlic, crushed

1/4 pint (142ml pot) double cream

1 tsp grainy mustard

1 tbsp brandy

Chopped parsley to finish

Prepare ahead:

No, serve as soon as it is ready

Freeze:

No

1   Put a deep sauté pan into the roasting oven to heat up for 5 minutes or so.

2   Transfer the pan to the boiling plate and put the steaks into it. Cook quickly, turning only once. When the steaks are cooked to your taste, remove from the pan and leave to rest. Approximate cooking times for a thick fillet steak: rare: 3–4 minutes each side, medium: 5–6 minutes each side.

3   Melt the butter in the pan, add the mushrooms and garlic and put onto the floor of the roasting oven, shaking the pan after a few minutes. The juices from the mushrooms should boil away. Transfer the pan to the simmering plate and add the brandy. Light a match on the boiling plate and set fire to the mushrooms. When the flames have died down, stir in the cream and mustard, pour over the steaks and serve at once, with a scattering of chopped parsley.

beef with noodles

To feed more people: Double the ingredients will feed 12 generously. For 16, use 12 steaks and three packets of noodles.

Serves 6

5 sirloin steaks

2 tbsp soy sauce

2 tsp runny honey

2 oz (55g) roasted cashew nuts

4 spring onions

1 pack (250g) thin rice noodles

2 tbsp grapeseed oil

1 tbsp sesame oil

1 clove garlic

1 red chilli

1 red pepper

3 tbsp beef stock

1 tbsp Thai fish sauce

Juice of a lime

Handful fresh basil leaves

Oven:

Boiling plate

Prepare in advance:

Chop all the ingredients ready to stir fry at the last minute

Prepare ahead:

Will keep warm in the simmering oven for up to half an hour, although the noodles may become a little solid

Freeze:

No, the noodles clog together in a big lump!

1   Fill the kettle and put it on to boil.

2   Put a wok or large heavy based pan into the roasting oven to heat up.

3   Trim the steaks of any fat and cut into thin slices.

4   Mix together the soy sauce and honey and add the meat, stir to coat and leave to marinate for a few minutes if possible.

5   Trim and slice the spring onions, crush the garlic, trim and slice the pepper and chop the chilli.

6   Put the noodles into a bowl and pour the boiling water over them. Leave to stand for 5 minutes, then drain.

7   Take the wok from the oven and set it on the boiling plate. Add the oils then add the meat, onions, garlic, chilli and pepper and stir fry for about 3 minutes.

8   Add the drained noodles, cashew nuts, stock, fish sauce and lime juice to the pan and continue to stir fry for another minute or so.

9   Serve sprinkled with torn basil leaves.

horseradish crusted roast beef

To feed more people: A larger joint will feed more people! Allow about 6 oz (175g) uncooked meat per person. The same size joint, with lots of Yorkshire puddings and several roast potatoes per person will feed up to 6.

Serves 4

2lb (1kg) roasting joint of beef, preferably topside or top rib

3 tbsp horseradish sauce or 1 tbsp grated fresh horseradish

1 tbsp fresh breadcrumbs

Salt and pepper

1 onion

For the gravy:

1 tbsp plain flour

1 pint (550ml) beef stock

1 tbsp red wine

Salt and pepper

Oven:

Roasting oven

Prepare in advance:

Make the crust and coat the beef up to 24 hours in advance

Prepare ahead:

Keep warm in warming oven for half an hour

Freeze:

Uncooked, coated meat. Cooked gravy will freeze, too.

1 Take the beef from the fridge at least an hour before you plan to roast it, to bring it up to room temperature – this makes for a crisper crust and does not suck too much heat from the Aga oven. If you are having Yorkshire puddings with the beef, cook them at this stage, while the Aga is at its hottest.

2 Mix together the horseradish, breadcrumbs and seasoning – it should be a thick paste. Smear the horseradish paste over the outside of the beef.

3 Weigh the beef and calculate the cooking time – for rare, allow about 12–15 minutes per pound, 25–30 minutes per kilo. For more well done, allow up to 18 minutes per pound, 40 minutes per kilo. For beef on the bone, add an extra 5 minutes to the total cooking time.

4 Peel and slice the onion and put into the bottom of the roasting tin, lined with Bake-O-Glide, then set the meat on top of the onion and roast it.

5 *Fast roasting*: Put the meat into the roasting oven for the full calculated cooking time.

6 *Medium roasting*: Put the meat into the roasting oven for one third of the calculated cooking time, then transfer to the simmering oven for the entire calculated time, ie. add a third to the length of time.

7 Once the beef is cooked to your liking, take it from the oven and put on a plate to rest while you make the gravy.

8 Pour away most of the fat from the tin, leaving the onion and meat juices in the tin. Stir in the flour and blend well. Stir in the wine and stock, until it is all well mixed. Season and stir.

9 Set the tin onto the floor of the roasting oven for the gravy to boil, while you reheat the Yorkshire puddings on the 2nd runners.

10 Stir the gravy and serve with the beef, together with Yorkshire puddings, roast potatoes and all the trimmings!

savoury yule log

To feed more people: This will give 10 slices to serve as an alternative to stuffing with Christmas dinner.

Serves 4–6

1 medium onion

1 clove garlic

1 tbsp olive oil

1 cooking apple

1 lb (450g) serious pork sausages

1 pack (200g) prepared chestnuts

2 tbsp parsley

1 tbsp fresh sage

1 egg

2 slices bread

Salt and pepper

4 oz (110g) fresh cranberries

12 slices streaky bacon

Oven:

Roasting oven, 200C, 400F, Gas 6

Prepare in advance:

Make the log and refrigerate for up to 24 hours before cooking

Prepare ahead:

Keep warm in simmering oven for up to an hour

Freeze:

Yes, before cooking

1   Peel and chop the onion, crush the garlic. Heat a pan on the simmering plate and add the onions and garlic. When sizzling, cover and transfer to the simmering oven for 10 minutes to soften.

2   Peel, core and grate the apples in a processor. Remove the skins from the sausages and add to the processor bowl, with the chestnuts, herbs, seasoning, bread and egg. When the onion and garlic are softened, add them to the processor and whizz the whole lot together, or mix thoroughly in a bowl.

3   Stretch the bacon with the back of a round ended knife and arrange in a rectangle on a large piece of foil. Spread the sausage mixture over the bacon, then scatter the cranberries over the top.

4   Lift one end of the foil and roll up into a tight log. Wrap the foil around the log and set into the small roasting tin.

5   Hang the tin from the 3rd runners in the roasting oven and bake for about 45 minutes. Unwrap the parcel and return to the oven for the bacon to brown – about 10 minutes.

6   Leave to stand and firm up for 10 minutes before serving carved into slices.

Ring the changes:

• Use the sausage mixture to make stuffing balls

• Substitute dried cranberries for fresh

• Substitute ready-to-eat dried apricots for the cranberries

moors and christians
(caribbean rice and beans)

The ham may not be traditional, but it adds a depth of flavour. Leave out if vegetarian!

To feed more people: Double the quantity should go around 10 people, especially if serving with another vegetable and a meaty main course.

Serves 4

1 can black peas (340g), drained

8 oz (225g) long grain rice

½ lb (225g) smoked cooked ham

2 tbsp olive oil

1 onion

2 cloves garlic

2 tomatoes

1 green pepper

3/4 pint (450ml) water or stock

Salt and pepper

1 tbsp chopped parsley

Oven:

Aga simmering oven, 130C, 250F, Gas 1

Prepare in advance:

Chill after cooking and store in fridge for up to 2 days

Prepare ahead:

Will keep warm in simmering oven for an hour or two

Freeze:

Yes

1 Peel and slice the onion, peel and crush the garlic.

2 Heat the oil in a heavy casserole and add the garlic and onions. When sizzling, cover and transfer to the simmering oven for 10 minutes to soften.

3 Chop the tomatoes and pepper and add to the pan, with the rice and drained beans. Cut the ham into small dice and add to the pan.

4 Add the water or stock, season and bring to the boil. Cover and transfer to the simmering oven for at least 20 minutes, but it will be fine for up to a couple of hours.

5 Serve scattered with chopped parsley.

pizza

To feed more people: Make two pizzas to feed three or four people, make one vast one with double the ingredients to feed 5.

Makes one

1 pack white bread mix

1 ball (200g) mozzarella cheese

4 oz (130g) Italian cured ham

2 oz (55g) mushrooms

4 tbsp tomato sauce (eg from pasta al sugo)

1 tbsp olive oil

1 Make up the bread mix according to the instructions on the packet.

2 Lay a sheet of Bake-o-Glide on the plain shelf, and roll out half of the bread dough onto it. Brush with oil, cover with cling film and leave near the Aga to rise for about 30 minutes.

pizza *continued*

Oven:

Roasting oven

Prepare in advance:

Prepared, chilled pizza will keep in
the fridge for up to 24 hours

Prepare ahead:

Cooked pizza will keep warm for
up to 30 minutes in simmering
oven

3 When ready to create your pizza, spread the risen
dough with a thin layer of tomato sauce, then scatter
over some torn-up ham, sliced mushrooms and
grated mozzarella cheese.

4 Put the shelf with the pizza on it onto the floor of the
roasting oven and bake for 15–20 minutes.

Freeze:

Yes, uncooked pizza

sweet and sour pork stir fry

To feed more people: Double the ingredients will feed up to 10, especially if
served with other main dishes.

Serves 4

1 lb (450g) thin pork steaks

1 pack (200g) sugar snap peas

4 oz frozen peas

1 onion

1 clove garlic

2 tbsp sunflower oil

1/2 jar / 4 tbsp mango chutney

1 tbsp cider vinegar

2 tbsp water

Oven:

Boiling plate

Prepare in advance:

Chop and assemble ingredients
and chill until needed

Prepare ahead:

Eat as soon as cooked if possible

Freeze:

No

1 Put a wok or heavy pan into the roasting oven to heat
up.

2 Trim the meat and cut into thin strips. Peel and slice
the onion and crush the garlic.

3 Heat the oil in the wok, then add the meat, onion and
peas. Stir fry for a couple of minutes until the meat is
cooked and the vegetables tender, then stir in the
garlic, mango chutney, vinegar and water.

4 Bring to the boil and serve at once, on a bed of rice.

tamarind pork rashers

To feed more people: Double the quantity of meat will need double the quantity of sauce to feed 8, but three times the amount of meat will only need double the sauce to feed 12.

Serves 4

8 pork belly rashers

2 tbsp tamarind paste

2 tbsp mango chutney

1 clove garlic

2 tbsp chopped fresh coriander to serve

Oven:

Roasting oven, 200C, 400F, Gas 6

Prepare in advance:

Leave the meat in the marinade in the fridge for up to 24 hours

Prepare ahead:

Will keep warm in simmering oven for half an hour

Freeze:

Yes, uncooked in the bag!

1 Peel and crush the garlic, then mix it with the tamarind paste and mango chutney.

2 Smear this sticky paste over the pork rashers and set aside to marinate for at least an hour.

3 Line the shallow baking tray with Bake-O-Glide and put the pork into it.

4 Hang the tin from the 2nd runners in the roasting oven and bake until golden and even stickier – about 20 minutes.

5 Serve with the coriander scattered over the top, with rice or spiced mashed potatoes.

Alternatives:

- Try using chicken thighs or even drumsticks instead of the pork

- Try using spare ribs instead of the belly rashers, but allow an extra rib per person as they are not as meaty as the rashers!

smart sausages

To feed more people: Double the quantity will feed 8, three times the sausages and double the sauce will feed 12.

Serves 4

8 thick sausages

1 tbsp olive oil

2 red onions

1 clove garlic

1 tbsp grainy mustard

4 oz (110g) seedless red grapes

2 tbsp red wine vinegar

Oven:

Floor of roasting oven

Prepare in advance:

Cooked, cooled sausages will keep in the fridge for 24 hours

Prepare ahead:

Keep warm in the simmering oven for an hour or so

Freeze: *Yes*

1 Peel and slice the onions and crush the garlic. Halve the grapes.

2 Heat the oil in a heavy based pan and add the sausages. Transfer to the floor of the roasting oven for 10 minutes to brown.

3 Take the pan from the oven, shake well to turn the sausages and add the onions, garlic and mustard. Return the pan to the floor of the roasting oven for a further 10 minutes, shaking it occasionally.

4 Once the sausages have browned and cooked, move the pan to the boiling plate and add the grapes and red wine vinegar. Season and boil for a couple of minutes until the sauce has thickened.

5 Serve with lots of mashed potato to absorb the sauce.

wallop sausage casserole

Perfect for bonfire night!

To feed more people: Double the quantity will feed 10, particularly if you cut the sausages into three pieces each.

Serves 4

1 lb (450g) chipolata sausages

1 onion

1 clove garlic

1 tbsp olive oil

2 parsnips

2 carrots

1 tbsp plain flour

1 tbsp grainy mustard

½ pint (300ml) stock

Salt and pepper

Oven:

Roasting oven, 200C, 400F, Gas 6 and simmering oven, 130C, 250F, Gas 1

Prepare in advance:

Cooked, cooled casserole will keep in fridge for up to 24 hours

Prepare ahead:

Keep warm in simmering oven for up to an hour

Freeze: *Yes*

1 Line the small roasting tin with Bake-O-Glide and put in the small grill rack, big feet down so that the rack is level with the top of the tin.

2 Set the sausages onto the rack and hang the tin from the 3rd runners in the roasting oven – cooking them away from the hot roof of the oven means you don't have to turn them as they roast! Cook for about 15 minutes until browned to your liking.

3 Peel and chop the onion and garlic. Cut the parsnips and carrots into even sized rounds.

4 Heat the oil in a heavy based pan on the simmering plate and add the vegetables. Stir around and, once sizzling, cover and transfer to the simmering oven for about 15 minutes to soften.

5 Take the pan of vegetables from the oven and stir in the flour and mustard, season well and pour on the stock, stirring until it is blended. Bring to the boil on the boiling plate then tip the sausages off their rack into the pan, leaving all the fat in the roasting tin.

6 Cover the pan and return it to the simmering oven for about half an hour. Or an hour. Or two hours, until you are ready to eat it.

7 Serve with mashed potatoes and a green vegetable.

If you cut each sausage into 3 before adding to the casserole, people will think that they are getting more than they really are, and the dish will stretch to 5 or 6!

slow shoulder of pork

To feed more people: A bigger joint will go further, and take extra time in the oven – a 3kg piece will feed up to 10, but may need 7 hours in the simmering oven.

Serves 6

4 lb (2kg) shoulder of pork

1 onion

1 tbsp olive oil

1 oz (25g) butter

1 tbsp ground ginger

2 rounds stem ginger

1 tbsp plain flour

2 cloves garlic

1 pint (550ml) cider

Salt and pepper

3 eating apples

4 oz (110g) chestnut mushrooms

Small pot (150ml) soured cream

Chopped parsley to garnish

Oven:

Simmering oven, 130C, 250F, Gas 1

Prepare in advance:

Keep the cooked cooled pork in the fridge for 24 hours

Prepare ahead:

Will keep in the simmering oven for an extra couple of hours

Freeze:

Yes

1 Peel and slice the onion and crush the garlic. Grate the stem ginger.

2 Heat the oil and butter in a heavy casserole, and add the pork joint. Set the pan on the floor of the roasting oven for 5 minutes to brown the meat, then remove from the oven, turn the meat over and return to the oven to brown the other side (you can do this on the top of the Aga, but it will spit fat all over the ironing and drying up!).

3 Take the pan from the oven, set it on the simmering plate and add the onions, garlic, grated stem ginger and ground ginger. Stir together, then pour on the cider. Season and bring to the boil.

4 Cover the pan and transfer to the simmering oven for about 6 hours until the meat is falling apart and tender.

5 Slice the apples off their cores and slice the mushrooms.

6 Remove the meat from the pan, and set it onto a plate to rest. Add the apples and mushrooms to the pan and put it, without its lid, onto the floor of the roasting oven for 10 minutes until the sauce has reduced and the vegetables are soft.

7 Just before serving, pour on the cream and stir to a swirl in the sauce. Scatter with parsley and serve.

pork pie

This is the easiest pastry in the world to make, crisp and delicious and it sits happily for hours in the Aga, cooking with no effort at all! The vegetable stock powder is an unusual addition, but it gives a wonderful depth of flavour to the meat.

To feed more people: Double the quantity will make a pie in a 8" / 20cms cake tin and will feed up to 9, triple the quantity will make a pie in a 10" / 27 cms tin and will feed up to 15, especially if served as part of a larger meal or picnic. But it will need at least an extra hour in the simmering oven to cook.

Serves 4

12 oz (350g) plain flour

4 oz (110g) lard or butter

8 tbsp water

Salt and pepper

1 lb (450g) pork casserole meat or belly rashers

8 oz (225g) bacon pieces

1 tbsp stock powder

Salt and pepper

1 egg, beaten

½ pint (300ml) good home made stock

Oven:

Baking oven, 180C, 375F, Gas 4, then simmering oven, 130C, 250F, Gas 1

Prepare in advance:

Cooked, cooled pie will keep in the fridge for 48 hours

Freeze:

Yes

1 Put the lard or butter and water into a pan and set on the simmering plate to melt together. Bring to the boil, then tip in the flour and beat into a dough.

2 Grease a 6" (15cms) cake tin and put in about two thirds of the pastry. Spread this out to cover the case and sides of the tin. Leave to cool, wrapping the remaining third of the pastry in cling film until needed.

3 Chop the pork and bacon into small dice. Mix with the stock powder and seasoning, and pile into the tin. Press down firmly, so that it all fits in.

4 Roll out the remaining pastry to make a lid for the pie – stick it on with some water and press down on the edges to seal, make a hole in the top for steam to escape, brush with beaten egg, then bake the pie.

5 *3 and 4 oven Aga*: put the grid shelf on the floor of the baking oven and set the tin onto it. Bake for about 1½ hours until well browned, then transfer to the simmering oven for a further hour to finish cooking.

6 *2 oven Aga*: Set the tin into the large roasting tin and hang from the 4th runners in the roasting oven, and slide the plain shelf onto the 2nd runners. Bake for about 50 minutes until well browned, then transfer the pie to the simmering oven for a further hour and a half to continue cooking without browning any more.

7 Take the pie from the oven and allow to cool a little.

8 While the pie is cooling, bring the stock to boiling point. Using a funnel, pour the stock into the hole in the centre of the pie to fill any gaps left when the meat shrank as it cooked.

9 Serve the pie cold, but not straight from the fridge.

lamb and rhubarb casserole

To feed more people: Double the quantity should give up to 10 portions.

Serves 4

1½ lb (650g) lamb neck fillet

1 clove garlic

1 onion

1 stem rhubarb

2 tsp ground cumin

Salt and pepper

1 tbsp plain flour

¼ pint (150ml) stock

1 large glass white wine

Oven:

Simmering oven, 250F, 130C, Gas 1 and floor of roasting oven

Prepare in advance:

Keep the cooked, cooled casserole in fridge for up to 24 hours and scrape any solidified fat off the top before reheating.

Prepare ahead:

Keep warm in simmering oven for up to an hour

Freeze:

Yes

1   Peel and slice the onion and rhubarb; crush the garlic.

2   Cut the meat into thin slices.

3   Heat the oil in a heavy casserole and add the meat, cumin, garlic, rhubarb and onions. Fry on the floor of the roasting oven until browned, shaking the pan occasionally to turn the meat.

4   Transfer the pan to the boiling plate and stir in the flour, then pour on the wine and stock. Stir until it boils, then cover and put into the simmering oven for about an hour.

Ring the changes:

- Substitute cinnamon and an apple for the rhubarb and cumin
- Substitute ground allspice and fresh apricots for the rhubarb and cumin

lamb biryani

To feed more people: Double the quantity should give up to 10 portions if served as part of a large curry meal with lots of accompaniments.

Serves 4–5

1½ lb (700g) lamb neck fillet

1 tbsp olive oil

8 oz (225g) (½ pint) long grain rice

¾ pint (425ml) stock or water

1 onion

1 clove garlic

1 tbsp Balti curry paste or 1 tbsp curry powder

8 oz (225g) spinach

Oven:

Simmering oven, 130C, 250F, Gas 1

Prepare in advance:

Cooked cooled Biryani will keep in fridge for up to 24 hours

Prepare ahead:

Keep warm in the simmering oven for an hour

Freeze:

Yes, defrost and reheat in roasting oven for 25 minutes

1 Cut the lamb into ½"/1cm slices. Peel and chop the onion, crush the garlic.

2 Heat the oil in a pan on the simmering plate and add the lamb, onion and garlic. Stir to mix then transfer the pan to the floor of the roasting oven to brown the meat for 5 minutes, shaking the pan once to turn the meat.

3 When the meat is brown, move the pan to the boiling plate and add the curry paste or powder. Stir over the heat for a minute then add the rice and stock, stirring until it has boiled. Cover and transfer to the simmering oven for at least 20 minutes.

4 Once the rice is cooked and has absorbed all the stock, add the spinach, re-cover the pan and return to the simmering oven for 5 minutes until the spinach has wilted.

5 Serve hot.

lamb rogan josh

To feed more people: Double the quantity will give up to 14 portions, especially if served as part of a large curry meal with other accompaniments.

Serves 6

2 lb boned leg of lamb

2" (5cm) piece root ginger

6 cloves garlic

4 tbsp water

3 tbsp vegetable oil

10 cardamom pods

6 cloves

2 bay leaves

10 peppercorns

1 stick cinnamon

2 onions

1 tsp ground coriander

2 tsp ground cumin

4 tsp paprika

1 tsp salt

½ tsp garam masala

½ pint (300ml) water

6 tbsp yogurt

4 oz (110g) cherry tomatoes

Fresh coriander to garnish

Oven:

Simmering oven, 250F, 130C, Gas 1 and floor of roasting oven

Prepare in advance:

Keep the cooked, cooled curry in fridge for up to 24 hours

Prepare ahead:

Keep warm in simmering oven for up to an hour

Freeze:

Yes

1   Put the ginger, garlic and 4 tbsp water into a small processor bowl and whizz to a paste.

2   Peel and slice the onions.

3   Cut the meat into 1" cubes.

4   Heat the oil in a heavy casserole and add the cubed meat and onions. Fry on the floor of the roasting oven until browned, shaking the pan occasionally to turn the meat.

5   Put the cardamom, bay leaves, cloves, peppercorns and cinnamon into a muslin bag or spice ball to contain them, then add to the pan.

6   Stir the ground spices and salt into the meat pan, then add the garlic and ginger paste. Stir over the heat, then stir in the yogurt, a tablespoon at a time, stirring continually.

7   Stir in the water, bring to the boil then cover and put into the simmering oven for 2 hours until the meat is tender. Remove the lid from the pan and transfer to the floor of the roasting oven to reduce and thicken the sauce – about 10 minutes.

8   Quarter the tomatoes and stir into the pan, then serve with a scattering of chopped fresh coriander.

italian lamb casserole

To feed more people: Double the quantity should give up to 10 portions, served with lots of rice.

Serves 4

1½ lb (650g) lamb neck fillets

2 tbsp olive oil

1 onion

2 cloves garlic

1 carrot

1 stick celery

1 sprig fresh rosemary

1 tbsp plain flour

¼ pint (150ml) white wine

1 tin (400g) chopped tomatoes

3 tbsp black olives (pitted)

1 lemon

1 tbsp chopped parsley to serve

Oven:

Simmering oven, 130C, 250F, Gas 1

Prepare in advance:

Refrigerate for 24 hours, remove any fat from the top before reheating

Prepare ahead:

Keep warm in simmering oven for an hour

Freeze:

Yes

1 Cut the lamb fillet into slices. Peel and chop the onion, crush the garlic and dice the carrot and celery. Chop the rosemary.

2 Heat a casserole or sauté pan on the simmering plate, add the oil, meat, onions, garlic, carrot and celery and transfer to the floor of the roasting oven for 5 minutes to brown. Give it a shake and return to the floor of the oven to continue browning for a further 5 minutes.

3 Take the pan of browned meat from the oven to the boiling plate, stir in the flour then add the wine and stir until boiling. Add the tomatoes, rosemary and olives. Grate in the rind of the lemon then squeeze in the juice. Season well and bring to the boil.

4 Cover the pan and transfer to the simmering oven for about an hour until the meat is tender.

5 Serve with a scattering of chopped parsley to show you have made an effort.

braised lamb shanks

To feed more people: Remove the cooked meat from the bones and cut it up – now you can divide it between up to 6 plates! If the shanks are especially large, 8 shanks will easily feed 12 people. Make sure there is lots of potato to soak up the sauce.

Serves 4

4 lamb shanks

1 jar (200ml) passata, sieved tomatoes OR 2 tins (340g each) tomatoes

½ pint (275ml) stock

½ pint (275ml) red wine

2 carrots

2 onions

1 leek

2 cloves garlic

1 oz (25g) butter

1 oz (25g) plain flour

1 sprig lemon thyme

Oven:

Simmering oven, 130C, 250F, Gas 1 and roasting oven, 200C, 400F, Gas 6

Prepare in advance:

Cooked, cooled casserole will keep in the fridge for up to 24 hours

Prepare ahead:

Keep warm in simmering oven for half an hour

Freeze:

Yes, defrost and reheat in the roasting oven for half an hour or so

1   Line a roasting tin with Bake-O-Glide. Set a grill rack into the tin and lay the lamb shanks into it. Hang the tin from the third set of runners in the roasting oven and cook the shanks for about 20 minutes until browned. Remove from the oven.

2   Peel and chop the onions, crush the garlic, trim and slice the leek and cut the carrots into ½"/1cm chunks.

3   Melt the butter in a heavy casserole on the simmering plate and add the vegetables. When sizzling, cover and transfer to the simmering oven for 15 minutes to soften.

4   Transfer the vegetable pan to the simmering plate and stir in the flour, then add the passata, stirring all the time, then add the stock and wine and the sprig of thyme.

5   Bring to the boil, season well and add the browned lamb shanks.

6   Cover and transfer to the simmering oven for about 2 hours until the meat is tender.

7   Remove the cooked lamb from the pot and put on a plate in the simmering oven to keep warm.

8   Transfer the pan, uncovered, to the floor of the roasting oven for about 15–20 minutes to thicken and reduce the sauce.

9   Put the meat back into the sauce and serve.

spiced shoulder
of lamb

This is a very cheap and filling casserole, which improves enormously if eaten the day after you have cooked it – keeping the cooled casserole in the fridge overnight means you can easily remove any fat that may have set on the top of the sauce and allows time for the flavours to develop fully.

To feed more people: A 3 lb (1.5kg) joint with the same amount of other ingredients will go around 8 people, double the sauce and a 4½ lb (2kg) joint will serve 12.

Serves 4

1½ lb (600g) boned lamb shoulder joint

1 onion

1 clove garlic

1 tbsp olive oil

10 peppadew peppers

6 sundried tomatoes

1 tin (400g) butter beans

½ pint (300ml) stock

1 tbsp plain flour

Salt and pepper

Oven:

Simmering oven, 130C, 250F, Gas 1

Prepare in advance:

Cooked, cooled meat will keep in the fridge for up to 48 hours – remove the fat from the top of the sauce before reheating

Prepare ahead:

Will keep warm in the simmering oven for an additional hour or so

Freeze:

Yes

1 Peel and chop the onion. Crush the garlic. Slice the peppadew peppers and sundried tomatoes. Open the tin of beans and drain, discarding the liquid.

2 Heat the oil in a large, heavy based pan on the boiling plate and add the onion, garlic and the piece of meat.

3 Transfer the pan to the floor of the roasting oven for 5 minutes to brown. Remove from the oven, turn the meat over and return to the floor of the oven to brown again for 5 minutes.

4 Move the pan to the boiling plate, stir in the flour then add the stock, stirring until it is well mixed and starting to boil. Add the peppadew peppers, tomatoes and the beans and season well.

5 When the sauce is boiling well, cover and transfer to the simmering oven for about 4 hours until the meat is meltingly tender: it should fall apart and not really need carving at all.

6 Serve with rice or mashed potatoes or a mixed mash or potatoes, sweet potatoes and celeriac or swede.

crunchy pear tart

To feed more people: Double the quantity will fill a 12"/30cms tin and you should get at least 16 portions.

Serves 6–8

For the pastry:

6 oz (175g) plain flour

3 oz (85g) butter

2 tbsp caster sugar

1 egg yolk

2 tbsp cold water

Filling:

5 ripe pears

Rind and juice of a lemon

1 oz (25g) soft brown sugar

½ tsp ground cinnamon

Topping:

3 oz (85g) butter

3 oz (85g) plain flour

3 oz (85g) soft brown sugar

1 tbsp chopped hazelnuts (optional)

1 lemon

Oven:

Floor of roasting oven, 200C, 400F, Gas 6

Prepare in advance:

Assemble the tart up to 24 hours in advance and refrigerate until ready to cook it

Prepare ahead:

Keep warm for a couple of hours on the back of the Aga

Freeze:

Yes

1 To make the pastry, whizz all the ingredients (except the water) together in a processor, then add the water a little at a time until it comes together as a dough. Roll out and line a 9"/23cms ceramic flan dish. Chill or freeze until needed.

2 Set the butter for the topping in a bowl beside the Aga to soften.

3 Peel, core and slice the pears and tip them into a bowl. Add the grated rind and juice of the lemon, the sugar and spices and mix together. Put into the prepared pastry case.

4 For the topping, put all the ingredients into a bowl and chop together with a round-ended knife, to make a chunky crumble mix (or whizz in a processor!).

5 Scatter the topping over the pears in the pastry case and bake the tart on the floor of the roasting oven for about 25 minutes until golden brown.

6 Serve warm with lots of thick cream.

You could ring the changes :
• Substitute dessert apples for the pears
• Add some dried cranberries or dried cherries for a sharper tart
• Mix the pears with blackcurrants for a lovely purple pudding
• Add some sliced rhubarb or a punnet of gooseberries (and a spoonful of cornflour to absorb and thicken the fruit juices) instead of the pears
• Add some chocolate chips to the topping
• Add a spoonful of porridge oats to the topping for a crisper tart.

chocolate and orange pudding

To feed more people: Double the mixture will fill a 2 litre / 4 pint bowl or two 1 litre/2 pint bowls and will feed up to 15. The bigger bowl will need an extra hour in the simmering oven.

Serves 4–6

3 oz (85g) butter

2 oz (55g) plain chocolate

6 oz (175g) wholemeal self raising flour

½ tsp baking powder

2 oz (55g) cocoa powder

5 oz (150g) light muscovado sugar

2 eggs

2 tbsp milk

Filling:

1 medium orange – thin skinned

3 oz (85g) butter

3 oz (85g) light muscovado sugar

Oven:

Simmering oven, 130C, 250F, Gas 1

Prepare in advance:

Will keep in fridge for up to 24 hours after cooking

Prepare ahead:

Keep warm for up to 2 hours in simmering oven

Freeze:

Yes

1 Set the butter in two separate bowls and put one beside the Aga to soften. Put the chocolate into the other bowl with the butter and set on the back of the Aga to melt.

2 Put the orange into a pan, cover with cold water and bring to the boil. Cover and transfer to the simmering oven for 15 minutes.

3 Mix together the melted butter and chocolate, flour, sugar, cocoa, eggs and milk.

4 Line a 2 pint/1 litre pudding basin with cling film.

5 Tip about $^2/_3$ of the sponge mixture into the prepared basin.

6 For the filling: Take the orange from the oven and prick all over with a fork. Drop it into the basin of chocolate mix. Mix the softened butter and extra sugar together and put onto the orange. Pour on the rest of the chocolate mixture.

7 Make a lid for the bowl with cling film.

8 Take a large pan and fill with about 1"/2.5cms water. Lower in the pudding basin. Cover.

9 Bring to the boil then transfer to the simmering oven for at least 2½ hours.

10 Serve with custard or cream. Or both.

chocolate and cranberry fudge pie

To feed more people: make a second pie. Two pies will feed up to 16 people. Double the ingredients will fill a 12"/30cms flan case which will give up to 15 portions.

Serves 6

6 oz (175g) plain flour

3 oz (75g) butter

1 oz (25g) cocoa

1 tbsp caster sugar

1 egg yolk

2 tbsp cold water

12 oz (375g pack) fresh cranberries

4 oz (110g) plain chocolate

3 eggs

3 oz (75g) soft brown sugar

2 oz butter

Oven:

Aga roasting oven, 200C, 400F, Gas 6

Prepare in advance:

Cook, cool and refrigerate for up to 24 hours

Prepare ahead:

Keep warm beside the Aga for an hour

Freeze:

Yes

1 To make the pastry, put the flour, sugar, butter, cocoa and egg yolk into a processor and whizz to the consistency of breadcrumbs. With the motor running, add the water a little at a time, until it forms a dough. Roll out and line a 9" (23cm) ceramic flan dish. Refrigerate until needed.

2 Set the chocolate and butter in a bowl on the back of the Aga to melt.

3 To assemble the tart, tip the cranberries into the pastry case. Mix together the chocolate, butter, sugar and eggs, then pour over the cranberries and set on the floor of the roasting oven. Bake for about 25 minutes, until the pastry is brown and the top risen a little and golden.

4 Dust with icing sugar and serve tepid with crème fraîche.

raspberry and lemon cake

Makes 12 squares but can be cut into smaller pieces if necessary.

To feed more people: Double the ingredients will fill the large roasting tin and will give 24 portions. Or more if you cut them smaller!

6 oz (175g) butter

6 oz (175g) caster sugar

4 tbsp lemon curd

3 eggs

6 oz (175g) self raising flour

3 tbsp natural yogurt

7 oz (200g) raspberries, fresh or frozen

Icing sugar to finish

Oven:

Baking oven, 180C, 375F, Gas 4

Prepare in advance:

Cooked, cooled cake will keep in a tin for a couple of days if you hide it well!

Prepare ahead:

Uncut cake will cool down slowly in its tin for a couple of hours beside the Aga to serve tepid

Freeze:

Yes

1 Set the butter in a bowl beside the Aga to soften for half an hour, if time allows.

2 Line the small roasting tin with Bake-O-Glide.

3 Add the, sugar, lemon curd, yogurt, eggs and flour to the bowl of butter and beat well. Gently fold the raspberries into the mixture – *if using frozen fruit, do not allow to defrost before adding or it will just go mushy. It may take an extra 5 minutes to cook through.*

4 Tip the cake mixture into the prepared tin and bake.

5 *2 oven Aga*: Set the small roasting tin full of cake mix into the large roasting tin and hang from the 4th, lowest runners in the roasting oven. Slide the plain shelf onto the 2nd runners above and bake for about 20 – 25 minutes until golden and firm.

6 *3 and 4 oven Aga*: Hang the tin from the 4th runners in the baking oven and bake for about 25 minutes until golden and firm.

7 Leave the cake to cool a little in the tin, then turn onto a wire rack, remove the Bake-O-Glide and cut into 12 squares. Serve as warm as possible, dusted with a little icing sugar and lots of vanilla ice cream

Variations:

- Try fresh, pitted cherries instead of the raspberries
- Try quartered, stoned, fresh damsons instead of the raspberries
- Try halved fresh strawberries instead of the raspberries, perhaps using orange curd instead of the lemon
- Substitute wholemeal self raising flour and half a teaspoon of baking powder instead of normal self raising for a healthy option

cilla's apple and lemon tart

To feed more people: Double the ingredients will fill a 12"/30cms tart case and should give more than 12 portions.

Serves 6

Pastry:

6 oz plain flour

3 oz butter

2 tbsp apple juice

1 oz (25g) caster sugar

Grated rind of half a lemon

Filling:

2 Bramley apples

4 oz (110g) caster sugar

Grated rind of half a lemon

Juice of one lemon

2 eggs

1 oz (25g) butter

Topping:

1 lemon

2 tbsp Demerara sugar

Oven:

Floor of roasting oven, 400F, 200C, Gas 6

Prepare in advance:

Make the pastry and the filling but keep separate until just before baking

Prepare ahead:

Keep warm in the simmering oven for half an hour

Freeze:

Yes

1 To make the pastry, whizz all the ingredients (except the apple juice) together in a processor and add the apple juice a little at a time until it comes together as a dough. Roll out and line a 9"/23cms ceramic flan dish. Chill or freeze until needed.

2 Set the butter on the back of the Aga to melt.

3 Peel the apples and grate them into a bowl. Add the sugar and lemon rind and juice. Add the eggs and melted butter and stir together.

4 Pour the filling into the pastry case. Slice the lemon for the topping and lay the slices onto the tart.

5 Sprinkle the Demerara sugar on top and bake on the floor of the roasting oven for about 25 minutes, until the pastry is browned and the filling puffed up and golden.

6 Serve with ice cream or cream, or both!

pineapple tarts

To feed more people: Double the quantity should make 10 tarts or unroll the pastry and set up to 12 pineapple rings on it and bake as one large tart to give 12 portions.

Serves 4

1 small pineapple

1 pack (375g) ready-rolled puff pastry

3 tbsp light brown sugar

2 oz (55g) butter

5 cardamom pods

Pinch ground allspice

Oven:

Roasting oven, 190C, 375F, Gas 5

Prepare in advance:

Once the sauce is cold, make up the tarts, cover and refrigerate for 24 hours

Prepare ahead:

Keep warm beside the Aga for 20 minutes at most, or the pastry goes soggy

Freeze:

No, the pineapple wilts as it defrosts

1 Peel and slice the pineapple. Remove the core from each slice.

2 Remove the cardamom seeds from their pods and crush with a pestle and mortar. Add the allspice and mix together.

3 Heat the sugar in a heavy pan on the simmering plate until it begins to turn brown. Remove from the heat and stir in the butter and spices. Allow to cool.

4 Unroll the pastry and cut into four circles about $1/2$"/1cm larger than the pineapple slices. Lay a slice of pineapple onto each circle of pastry and tuck the edges up the sides of the pineapple to make a rim for each tart.

5 Spoon a quarter of the sauce over each tart, filling the hole where the core was.

6 Line the cold plain shelf with Bake-O-Glide and set the tarts onto it, then slide the shelf onto the floor of the roasting oven and bake for 15 minutes. Serve as they cool, with cream. Lots of it.

This works well with pretty much any firm fruit – slices of peach, nectarine, plum, apple, pear, you name it, it can be turned into a tart.

Change the spices depending upon the fruit – try apple and cinnamon, plum and almond extract, peach and ginger.

chocolate goo pudding

To feed more people: Double the mixture will fill up to 14 ramekins. Set them in the large roasting tin and bake for about 15 minutes.

Serves 6

4 oz (110g) butter

4 oz (110g) plain chocolate

4 oz (110g) soft brown sugar

1 oz (25g) plain flour

3 eggs

Oven:

Roasting oven, 200C, 400F, Gas 6

Prepare in advance:

Puddings will keep in fridge up to 24 hours (in fact they are delicious uncooked and raw!)

Freeze:

Yes, cook for 15 minutes from frozen

1   Break up the chocolate and set it in a bowl with the butter on the back of the Aga to melt for about 20 minutes.

2   Mix together the flour, sugar and eggs. Mix into the chocolate and butter.

3   Grease 6 ramekin dishes. Pour the chocolate mixture into the ramekins and set them in the small roasting tin to keep them together in the oven.

4   Hang the tin on the 4th runners in the roasting oven and cook for 10 minutes until slightly puffed up and not set, as they should be very soft in the centre.

5   Serve with a blob of cold yogurt or crème fraîche.

foolproof hot lemon soufflé

To feed more people: Double the quantity will fill 12 ramekins.

Serves 4–5

1 oz (25g) butter

1 tbsp caster sugar

4 egg whites

2 lemons

1/4 pint (150ml) custard – ready made in a tub is easiest!

Oven:

Aga roasting oven, 200C, 400F, Gas 6

1   Melt the butter in a ramekin on the back of the Aga.

2   Brush 3 or 4 other ramekins with the melted butter.

3   Divide the sugar between the ramekins and shake about to coat the butter with sugar – this helps the soufflé to rise evenly.

4   Grate the rind of the lemons and squeeze the juice. Put into a bowl with custard.

5   Whisk the egg whites and fold into the lemon custard.

6   Pour the mixture into the prepared ramekins and put them into the small shallow baking tray.

foolproof hot lemon soufflé *continued*

Prepare in advance:

Make the soufflés and refrigerate
until just before baking

Prepare ahead:

No, serve as soon as they come
out of the oven!

Freeze:

Uncooked, then add 5 minutes to
baking time from frozen

7   Hang the tray from the 3rd runners in the roasting
oven and bake for about 15 minutes until puffed up
and golden.

8   Serve at once, dusted with icing sugar.

park farm
lemon pudding

To feed more people: Double the ingredients will fill the small roasting tin and
should give up to 10 portions.

Serves 4

5 oz (150g) icing sugar

2 eggs

Grated rind of 2 lemons

Juice of 4 lemons

2$\frac{1}{2}$ oz (80g) ground almonds

3$\frac{1}{2}$ oz (100g) butter

Oven:

Grid shelf on floor of roasting oven
or centre of baking oven, 180C,
350F, Gas 4

Prepare in advance:

Assemble the dish and refrigerate
for up to 4 hours before cooking.

Prepare ahead:

Keep warm in the simmering oven
for up to half an hour

Freeze:

Yes

1   Put the butter in a bowl on the back of the Aga to
melt while you grate the lemon rind and squeeze the
juice.

2   Mix all the ingredients together and pour into an oven
proof dish.

3   *3 and 4 oven Aga*: Hang the grid shelf from the 4th
set of runners in the baking oven and cook the
pudding on that for about 25 minutes until risen and
golden.

4   *2 oven Aga*: set the grid shelf on the floor of the
roasting oven and cook the pudding on that for about
20 minutes. Slide the cold shelf onto the second set
of runners to protect the top of the pudding from
browning too fast.

5   Serve with cream

hazel's raspberry
brioche pudding

To feed more people: Double the quantity will fill a dish the size of the large roasting tin and will make enough for up to 15.

Serves 6–8

1 tbsp butter

1 loaf brioche

1 pack (100g) white chocolate drops

1 pack (350g) raspberries fresh or frozen

3 eggs

2 tbsp sugar

1 tub (200g) crème fraîche

Oven:

Baking oven, 170C, 375F, Gas 4

Prepare in advance:

Soaked brioche will keep in the fridge for up to 24 hours

Prepare ahead:

Keep warm in the simmering oven for up to an hour

Freeze:

Don't see why not!

1 Grease a large oven proof dish with the butter.

2 Cut the loaf in half and tear one half into medium sized chunks and scatter them over the base of the dish.

3 Scatter the chocolate drops over the brioche, then tip the raspberries over the top.

4 Tear the remainder of the loaf into chunks and scatter them over the raspberries.

5 Mix the eggs, sugar and crème fraîche together and pour over the brioche. Leave to stand for an hour, if possible, then bake.

6 *2 oven Aga*: Set the grid shelf on the floor of the roasting oven and put the dish onto it. Slide the plain shelf onto the 3rd runners and bake for about 25 minutes until puffed up and golden.

7 *3 and 4 oven Aga*: Hang the grid shelf on the 4th runners and put the dish onto it. Bake for about 25 minutes until puffed up and golden.

8 Serve warm with more crème fraîche, rather than piping hot, as the raspberries are VERY hot when they come out of the oven.

pear, cranberry and almond strudel

To feed more people: Make two strudels to produce 10 portions. Three will feed 18.

Serves 4

5 ripe pears

4 oz (110g) dried cranberries

1 lemon

½ tsp ground allspice

1 tbsp cornflour

2 tbsp caster sugar

2 oz (50g) flaked almonds

6 sheets filo pastry

1 oz (25g) butter

Oven:

Baking oven, 180C, 375F, Gas 5

Prepare in advance:

Uncooked strudel will keep in fridge for up to 24 hours

Prepare ahead:

Keep warm in simmering oven for half an hour

Freeze:

Uncooked strudel – freeze on the plain shelf then wrap once frozen. Can be cooked from frozen or defrosted.

1. Set the butter in a bowl on the back of the Aga to melt.

2. Peel, core and slice the pears. Tip into a large bowl with the grated rind and juice of the lemon and the dried cranberries. Add the allspice, cornflour, almonds and half of the sugar. Mix well.

3. Lay a sheet of Bake-O-Glide on the plain shelf and lay two sheets of filo pastry onto it, so that they overlap into a long rectangle. Brush with melted butter.

4. Lay two more sheets of filo on top of the buttered pastry, with the join not directly over the first join. Brush with melted butter.

5. Lay the remaining pastry sheets over the top. Spoon the filling onto the pastry, spreading it to within an inch of the edges.

6. Roll up the pastry into a long sausage, leaving the join underneath. Brush with the rest of the butter and scatter over the remaining sugar. Make diagonal cuts into the strudel, to stop the pastry collapsing as it shrinks in the oven.

7. *2 oven Aga*: Hang the shelf from the lowest runners in the roasting oven, with the large roasting tin on the top runners (acting as a plain shelf to protect the top of the strudel as it cooks). Bake for about 30 minutes until golden, then transfer to the simmering oven for another 20 minutes.

8. *3 and 4 oven Aga*: Hang the shelf from the lowest runners in the baking oven and cook for about 45 minutes until golden.

9. Sprinkle the strudel with icing sugar and serve warm, with cream.

raspberry frangipane tart

To feed more people: Double the quantity will fill a 12"/30cms flan dish and should give at least 12 portions

Serves 6

6 oz (175g) plain flour

3 oz (75g) butter

1 oz (25g) caster sugar

1 egg yolk

2 tbsp cold water

½ tsp almond extract

½ jar (about 4 tbsp) Bonne Maman raspberry conserve

2 eggs

1 tub (150g) mascarpone cheese

2 oz (55g) ground almonds

3 oz (75g) caster sugar

2 oz (55g) flaked almonds

Oven:

Roasting oven, 400F, 200C, Gas 6

Prepare ahead:

24 hours

Freeze:

Yes

1   To make the pastry, put the flour, sugar, butter, almond extract and egg yolk into a processor and whizz to the consistency of breadcrumbs. With the motor running, add the water a little at a time, until it forms a dough. Roll out and line a 9" (23cm) ceramic flan dish. Refrigerate until needed.

2   Put the tub of cheese onto the back of the Aga to soften.

3   To assemble the tart, spread the raspberry jam over the base of the pastry case. Mix together the egg yolk, mascarpone, sugar and almonds. Whisk the whites and fold in to the mixture, then pour over the raspberry base, scatter on the flaked almonds and set onto the floor of the roasting oven. Bake for about 25 minutes, until the pastry is brown and the top risen a little and golden.

4   Dust with icing sugar and serve tepid with crème fraîche.

Variation:

• Try using fresh raspberries instead of the conserve (or as well as!)

• Try using cherries, cherry compote or cherry conserve instead of the raspberry

• Try using a dozen fresh figs instead of raspberries or jam

honey and ginger peaches

To feed more people: Double the quantity will feed 8. 12 peaches and double the quantity of other ingredients will feed 12.

Serves 4

4 ripe peaches

2 tbsp runny honey

1 tsp vanilla powder or extract

1 lime

½ pint (284ml pot) cream

1 ball stem ginger

1 tbsp syrup from the ginger jar

Oven:

Roasting oven, 200C, 400F, Gas 6

Prepare in advance:

Refrigerate cooked, cooled peaches for up to 24 hours

Prepare ahead:

Keep peaches warm for half an hour

Freeze:

Flavoured cream only, the peaches will collapse when they defrost!

1 Grate the rind from the lime and squeeze the juice.

2 Mix together the honey, vanilla and lime rind and juice.

3 Line the small shallow baking tray with Bake-O-Glide.

4 Halve the peaches, remove the stones and lay the peach halves into the tin, cut side uppermost.

5 Dribble the honey mixture over the peaches and hang the tin from the lowest set of runners in the roasting oven – bake for about 20 minutes.

6 Whip the cream. Grate the stem ginger then fold it, with the syrup, into the cream.

7 Serve the hot peaches with the chilled cream.

hazelnut biscuits

To feed more people: Double the quantity will give at least 30 biscuits. Bake in two or three batches.

Makes about 15

2 oz (55g) hazelnuts

4 oz (110g) butter

2 oz (55g) caster sugar

5 oz (150g) plain flour

1 Set the butter in a bowl beside the Aga to soften. Line a shallow baking tray with Bake-O-Glide.

2 Put the nuts into a processor and grind to a lumpy powder. Tip the ground nuts into a heavy based pan and toast them on the boiling plate for a few minutes until golden. Watch them like a hawk, they will change colour very quickly!

hazelnut biscuits *continued*

Oven:

Lowest runners in roasting oven or centre of baking oven, 190C, 375F, Gas 5

Prepare in advance:

Biscuits will keep in an airtight tin for several days – if you hide the tin!

Freeze:

Yes

3 Tip the nuts into a bowl and leave them to cool.

4 Put the soft butter, cool nuts, sugar and flour into a processor and whizz into a dough.

5 Shape the dough into balls about the size of a walnut, then set them on the baking tray.

6 *2 oven Aga*: Hang the tray from the lowest runners in the roasting oven with the cold shelf on the 2nd set of runners.

7 *3 and 4 oven Aga*: Hang the tray from the 3rd set of runners in the baking oven.

8   Bake for about 10 minutes until golden brown. Cool on a wire rack, sprinkle with icing sugar and serve.

cardamom custard tart

To serve more people: Make two tarts, which will go around 10 – 12 people, more if there is another pudding, or double the ingredients will fill a 12" / 30cms tart case which should give up to 15 portions.

Serves 4–6

6 oz (175g) plain flour

1 oz (25g) caster sugar

3 oz (75g) butter

2 tbsp cold water

Filling:

7 oz (200g) tub natural yogurt

¼ pint (150ml) creamy milk

4 oz (110g) caster sugar

3 eggs

6 cardamom pods

Oven:

Roasting oven

Prepare in advance:

Make the custard and bake the

tart on the day it is to be eaten

Prepare ahead:

Tart will keep for up to an hour

beside the Aga, gently cooling

Freeze:

Yes: make the pastry and roll it out and line the dish,

then freeze it, uncooked, until needed.

1 Put the milk and yogurt into a bowl with the sugar and set on the back of the Aga to warm. Open the cardamom pods, remove the seeds and crush them. Stir into the milk mixture.

2 To make the pastry, whizz the flour, caster sugar and butter in a processor. Add sufficient water to bind into dough. Roll out and line a 9"/23cm flan dish. Chill for at least half an hour.

3 Beat the eggs and add to the yogurt and milk mixture. Pour into the pastry case.

4 Bake on the floor of the roasting oven for 25 minutes. Serve warm.

cilla's upside down toffee pudding

To feed more people: Double the ingredients will fill the large roasting tin and will give 10 to 12 portions

Serves 4–5

Pudding:

4 oz (110g) dark brown sugar

6 oz (175g) wholemeal self raising flour

¼ pint (150ml) milk

1 egg

1 tsp vanilla extract

2 oz (55g) butter

8 oz (225g) chopped dates or sultanas

Sauce:

7 oz (200g) dark brown sugar

1 oz (25g) butter

1 pint (550ml) boiling water

Oven:

Grid shelf on floor of roasting oven, or centre of baking oven, 180C, 350F, Gas 4

Prepare in advance:

Assemble the pudding an hour before baking

Prepare ahead:

Keep warm in the simmering oven for half an hour

Freeze:

Yes

1   Set the butter and milk in a bowl on the back of the Aga to melt for about 20 minutes.

2   Mix the sugar, flour, vanilla and dates together. Pour on the warm milk and butter and add the egg.

3   Beat together and pour into an ovenproof dish.

4   Mix together the sauce ingredients and pour over the pudding.

5   *3 and 4 oven Aga*: set the dish on the grid shelf on the 4th runners and bake for about 45 minutes.

6   *2 oven Aga*: set the dish on the grid shelf on the floor of the roasting oven and slide the cold shelf onto the 2nd runners. Bake for about 30–35 minutes.

7   Serve with ice cream or cream, or both!

vanilla soufflé

To feed more people: Double the ingredients will fill 14 to 16 ramekins if you are not too generous. Don't try to make a single, vast soufflé to feed 12 as it will almost certainly collapse and will be runny in the centre when browned and risen on top. Stick to ramekins for a crowd!

Serves 6

2¼ oz (60g) butter

2 oz (55g) plain flour

1 pint (550ml) milk

4 eggs

4 oz (110g) caster sugar

2 tbsp vanilla extract

Oven:

Roasting oven, 200C, 400F, Gas 6

Prepare in advance:

The prepared soufflé will keep in the fridge for up to 24 hours, but cook it at the last minute!

Prepare ahead:

Eat as soon as it is ready.

Freeze:

Yes, uncooked – make the soufflé up to the point of going into the oven, pour into prepared ramekins, cover with cling film and freeze. To cook, remove the film, set the dishes in a roasting tin and hang from the 3rd runners in the roasting oven for about 20 minutes until defrosted, puffed up and browned.

1   Melt the butter in a pan on the simmering plate. Using a pastry brush, grease six ramekin dishes (or a 2 pint soufflé dish) with melted butter. Put some caster sugar into each ramekin and shake around so that it sticks to the butter.

2   Add the flour to the remaining butter in the pan and once mixed, stir in the sugar, vanilla extract and milk. Bring to the boil on the simmering plate, stirring all the time as this is a very thick sauce. Set on one side to cool a little.

3   Separate the eggs and stir the yolks into the sauce, one at a time. Whisk the egg whites until stiff, then fold in to the vanilla sauce.

4   Pour into the prepared dishes and set in the small roasting tin. Hang the tin from the third set of runners in the roasting oven for 15 minutes (if in one big dish, cook for 25 minutes) until puffed up and golden.

5   Serve immediately before it collapses!

strawberry soufflés

This is the most amazingly forgiving soufflé – there is no egg yolk and so it will not sink. You can prepare the soufflés hours in advance and bake them just before serving, or they will keep warm, cooked, for up to half an hour without sinking

To feed more people: Double the ingredients will fill up to 14 ramekins

Serves 6

4 tbsp Bonne Maman strawberry conserve

1 tbsp butter

4 oz (110g) caster sugar

4 egg whites

To finish:

1 tbsp icing sugar

Oven:

Aga roasting oven, 400F, 200C, Gas 6

Prepare ahead:

Mix up to an hour beforehand, but cook at the last minute

Freeze:

No

1   With a piece of kitchen paper and some butter, grease the inside of 6 ramekin dishes. Put the dishes into the small roasting tin.

2   Whisk the egg whites until stiff, then whisk in the sugar, a spoonful at a time, until it is thick and glossy.

3   Fold in the strawberry conserve, then pour into the prepared ramekin dishes. Hang the tin from the 3rd runners in the roasting oven and bake for 12–15 minutes until golden and puffed up. Dust with icing sugar and serve at once.

Ring the changes:
• Use marmalade instead of the strawberry jam
• Use lemon curd instead of the strawberry jam
• Use any fresh fruit puree instead of the strawberry jam

tiramisu

To feed more people: Double the ingredients will make a larger tiramisu to feed up to 12, or more if served with another pudding

Serves 4–6

½ pint (300ml) strong black coffee, cooled

2 oz (55g) caster sugar

6 tbsp Amaretto liqueur

2 eggs, separated

9 oz (250g tub) mascarpone cheese

1   Set the mascarpone tub on the back of the Aga to soften.

2   Mix the cold coffee with three tablespoons of the Amaretto and put to one side. Spread the biscuits over the base of a serving dish. Sprinkle about half of the coffee and liqueur mixture over the biscuits.

3   Beat together the egg yolks and sugar until thick and pale. Add the mascarpone and beat together. Fold in the whipped cream.

tiramisu *continued*

½ pint (284ml pot) whipped cream

cocoa powder, to dust

1 packet sponge finger biscuits

4   Whisk the egg whites. Fold into the cream mixture. Add the remaining liqueur.

5   Spread the cream mixture over the biscuits.

6   Smooth the surface and dust the top with the cocoa powder.

summer chocolate pots

To feed more people: Double the ingredients should fill 20 ramekins

Serves 8

½ pint (275ml pot) cream

2 heads of lavender flowers, or sprigs of rosemary

7½ oz (200g) plain chocolate

½ pint (250ml tub) natural yogurt

2 egg yolks

1 oz (25g) butter

8 additional lavender sprigs to serve

Oven:

Back of Aga, simmering plate

Prepare in advance:

Pots will keep in the fridge for up to 48 hours

Freeze:

Yes

1   Put the chocolate and butter in a bowl and set it in the back of the Aga to melt.

2   Put the cream and lavender into a pan and heat gently on the simmering plate. Do not boil. Remove from the heat and leave to infuse on the back of the Aga, while the chocolate melts.

3   Beat the egg yolks into the melted chocolate, then strain on the cream, followed by the yogurt, stirring all the time.

4   Pour the mixture into 8 small ramekins or coffee cups, cool and chill for a couple of hours.

5   Serve at room temperature if possible, with a lavender flower on top.

deborah miller's
white chocolate bliss

To feed more people: This is very rich and will serve up to 8. Double the ingredients will serve up to 20, especially if served with a fresh fruit salad.

Serves 6

8 oz (225g) white chocolate, broken into pieces

3/4 pint (450ml) double cream

3 egg whites

3 oz (75g) ratafia biscuits, coarsely crushed

3 oz (75g) roasted hazelnuts, coarsely chopped

Oven:

Back of the Aga to melt the

chocolate

Prepare in advance:

Will keep in the fridge for up to 24

hours, if well disguised

Freeze: *Yes*

1 Set the chocolate in a bowl on the back of the Aga to melt for about half an hour. Get the cream out of the fridge and whip it, leaving it at room temperature.

2 Pour the melted chocolate into the cream and fold together. Whisk the egg whites until stiff and fold into the cream mixture.

3 Spoon half the cream mixture into the base of a pretty serving bowl, about 2 pints/1 litre.

4 Sprinkle over half the crushed biscuits and hazelnuts.

5 Spoon over the remaining mixture, level the top and sprinkle over the remaining biscuits and nuts.

6 Chill for an hour or so, but serve at room temperature.

raspberry coulis

1 Whiz an 8 oz (225g) bag of frozen raspberries (or forest fruits) in a food processor.

2 Add 2 tablespoons of icing sugar and 1 tablespoon of water, to make a purée.

3 Sieve and then use as coulis.

4 Either pour it on the plate first and place a helping of the pudding on top, or hand it around so guests can add their own.

panna cotta

To feed more people: Double the panna cotta ingredients can fill 14 ramekins. Double the sauce will make 14 portions too.

Serves 6

1 pint (568ml) single cream

1 vanilla pod

1 tsp vanilla extract

3 oz (85g) caster sugar

1 tbsp Marsala (or orange juice)

1 tbsp water

1 tbsp powdered gelatine

Sauce:

1 lb (450g) raspberries or half raspberries and half strawberries

2 tbsp icing sugar

Oven:

Simmering plate

Prepare in advance:

The creams will keep in the fridge for up to 24 hours.

Freeze:

No, the cream will separate on defrosting.

1 Put the Marsala (or orange juice) and water into a jam jar and sprinkle on the gelatine. Leave for a couple of minutes until dissolved, then set in a pan of boiling water on the simmering plate to melt.

2 Put the cream, vanilla pod, vanilla extract and sugar into a pan and heat on the simmering plate, stirring until the sugar has dissolved. Bring to the boil. Allow to cool for a few minutes then tip the hot cream onto the gelatine – through a sieve – and stir well.

3 Oil 6 ramekins and line the bases with paper jam pot covers or cling film (to ensure they turn out!). Pour the cream into the prepared ramekins, cool, then chill for at least 4 hours.

4 Push 8oz (225g) of the raspberries through a sieve and stir in the icing sugar. (Or open a jar of raspberry coulis . . .)

5 Run a knife around the set creams, turn out and serve with the whole raspberries and raspberry sauce. Don't forget to peel off the papers!

Alternatives:

• Use a defrosted bag of summer fruits or forest fruits for the sauce if fresh fruit is unavailable.

lemon and honey roulade

To feed more people: Roll the roulade along its long edge for 10 portions from a single roulade! Make a second roulade and you should get up to 18 portions.

Serves 6

5 eggs

5 oz (150g) caster sugar

2 oz (55g) ground almonds

2 oz (55g) self raising flour

1 lemon

1/2 pint (275ml) cream

1 tbsp runny honey

Icing sugar to finish

Prepare in advance:

Will keep in fridge for up to 24 hours

Freeze:

Yes, wrapped in kitchen paper to absorb any moisture that comes off as it defrosts

1   Line the large roasting tin with Bake-O-Glide.

2   Separate the eggs. Grate the rind from the lemon and squeeze the juice.

3   Whisk the whites until stiff. Whisk the egg yolks and sugar until light and fluffy. Whisk in the grated lemon rind and the juice.

4   Fold the almonds and flour into the mixture, then fold in the egg whites.

5   Pour into the tin, spread evenly and bake.

6   *3 and 4 oven Aga* – Hang the tin from the lowest runners in the baking oven for about 20 minutes until risen and golden.

7   *2 oven Aga* – Hang the tin from the lowest runners in the roasting oven and slide the cold shelf onto the 2nd runners for about 15 minutes until risen and golden.

8   Take the cake from the oven and turn it out onto a clean tea towel. Remove the Bake-O-Glide and roll the roulade in the towel and leave to cool.

9   When the roulade is cool, whip the cream and stir in the honey. Spread this over the unrolled roulade, then re-roll it. Chill for an hour before serving, dusted with icing sugar.

Ring the changes:

• Try using oranges instead of the lemons, and marmalade instead of the honey for an orange roulade.

passion fruit
cheesecake

To feed more people: Double the ingredients will make a tart in a 12"/30cms flan dish and should give at least a dozen portions

Serves 4 – 5

6 oz (175g) plain flour

1 oz (25g) caster sugar

3 oz (75g) butter

2 tbsp cold water

Grated rind of a lemon

6 passion fruit

2 packs (400g) cream cheese

3 eggs

6 oz (175g) caster sugar

1 tub (200g) crème fraîche

Oven:

Aga roasting oven, 200C, 400F, Gas 6

Prepare in advance:

Make the tart and chill for up to 48 hours before needed

Freeze:

Yes

1 To make the pastry, whizz the flour, caster sugar, lemon rind and butter in a processor. Add sufficient water to bind into dough. Roll out and line a 9"/23cm flan dish. Chill for at least half an hour.

2 Set the packs of cream cheese onto the back of the Aga to soften.

3 Halve the passion fruit and put the pulp of 5 of them into a processor and whizz, then strain the juice through a sieve into a bowl. (If you like the hard pips, don't bother straining the juice!).

4 Add the sugar, eggs and soft cream cheese to the passion fruit juice and beat together. Pour into the prepared pastry case.

5 Cook the tart on the floor of the roasting oven for about 25 minutes, until the pastry is golden and the filling set and puffed up a little.

6 Remove from the oven and allow to cool for about an hour (it will sink to a flat top!), then spread the crème fraîche over the cool tart.

7 Scrape the pulp from the remaining passion fruit over the tart. Serve at room temperature.

cranberry and orange cheesecake

To feed more people: Double the quantity will fill a 12" metal based flan tin and makes up to 12 portions

Serves 6 greedy people!

Base:

10 Plain digestive biscuits

2 oz (50g) butter

1 oz (25g) soft brown sugar

Filling:

Grated rind of an orange

Juice of an orange

Tub (200g) mascarpone cheese

5 oz (150g) caster sugar

2 oz (50g) plain flour

2 eggs

Topping:

2 oz (50g) caster sugar

8 oz (225g) cranberries

2 tbsp orange juice

Oven:

Baking oven, 180C, 350F, Gas 4

Prepare in advance:

Cheesecake will keep in the fridge for up to 48 hours but do not serve straight from the fridge

Prepare ahead:

Keep the cheesecake warm beside the Aga for an hour or so before serving.

Freeze:

Yes

1   Set the butter in a bowl on the back of the Aga to melt, with the tub of mascarpone.

2   For the base, whizz all ingredients together in a processor.

3   Line the base of an 8"/20cms springform tin with Bake-O-Glide and tip in the base. Press down firmly.

4   Pile the filling ingredients into the processor bowl and whizz together. Pour into the tin.

5   *3 and 4 oven Aga*: Put the grid shelf on the floor of the baking oven and set the tin onto it and bake for 20 – 30 minutes until golden.

6   *2 oven Aga*: Set the tin into the large roasting tin and hang it from the lowest runners in the roasting oven, with the cold shelf on the 2nd runners. Cook for about 20–30 minutes until golden.

7   For the topping, put the cranberries, sugar and orange juice into a pan, bring to the boil then cover and transfer to the simmering oven for about 15 minutes until softened. If very liquid, remove the lid and put the pan onto the floor of the roasting oven for 5 minutes to reduce.

8   Allow to cool in the tin, then spread over the cranberry and orange topping. Serve warm as a pudding with some natural yogurt, or cold for tea.

lemon and lime cream

To feed more people: Double the quantity will fill up to 12 ramekins or 15 small espresso cups – it is quite rich, so small portions make sense.

Serves 6

1 lemon

1 lime

6 oz (175g) caster sugar

1/2 pint (284ml pot) double cream

1 tub (250g) mascarpone

Oven:

Simmering plate

Prepare in advance:

Will keep for 48 hours in the fridge

Freeze:

Yes

1　Squeeze the juice from the lemon and lime.

2　Set the mascarpone in its tub on the back of the Aga to soften.

3　Put the cream and sugar into a pan and heat gently on the simmering plate until the sugar has dissolved and the cream is not quite boiling.

4　Beat the mascarpone into the hot cream, then beat in the lemon and lime juice.

5　Pour into 6 ramekins or espresso cups, allow to cool, then chill for a couple of hours.

6　Serve with a big bowl of strawberries.

lemon mousse in chocolate cases

To feed more people: Make this quantity in an 8"/20cms deep cake tin, lined with the chocolate to feed 8. Double the quantity will fill a 10"/25cms tin or 16 ramekins.

Serves 6

For the case:

7 oz (200g) plain chocolate

For the mousse:

2 large lemons

4 oz (110g) caster sugar

3 eggs

1/2 pint (284 ml) double or whipping cream

1 tbsp powdered gelatine

1 tbsp icing sugar to serve

Oven:

Back of Aga

Prepare in advance:

Finished mousses will keep in fridge for up to 24 hours

Freeze:

Yes

1   Break up the chocolate and set it in a bowl on the back of the Aga to melt.

2   For individual cases: Line 6 ramekin dishes with cling film and carefully brush the insides with melted chocolate. Refrigerate for half an hour until set, then brush with another layer of chocolate. Refrigerate or freeze until needed.

3   For a single large case: Line the side and base of an 8" / 20cms springform tin with Bake-O-Glide and brush with melted chocolate. Refrigerate for half an hour until set, then brush with another layer of chocolate. Refrigerate or freeze until needed.

4   For the lemon mousse: Wash and dry the lemons then grate the rind into a large bowl. Squeeze the juice of the lemons into a smaller bowl.

5   Sprinkle the gelatine over the lemon juice and leave to stand for a minute, then set the bowl into a pan of simmering water to melt.

6   Separate the eggs and put the yolks into the bowl with the lemon rind, together with the sugar. Put the egg whites into another large bowl, and the cream into a third bowl – the large pile of washing up looks a bit daunting afterwards, but the pudding is worth it!

7   Whip the egg whites, then the cream, which should be thickened but not stiff. Then whisk the egg yolks, lemon rind and sugar until thick and pale. (No need to wash the beaters if you do it in the right order, creating a little less washing up.)

8   Take the chocolate cases from the fridge and carefully remove from the ramekins or tin. Set onto a serving plate.

9   Whisk the lemon juice and gelatine into the yolk mixture, leave to cool for a few minutes then fold in the cream and whisked whites. Pour into the prepared chocolate cases and chill until needed.

10 Serve with icing sugar sifted over the top to show that you have made an effort.

Ring the changes:
- Use white chocolate and oranges instead of the dark chocolate and lemons
- Use the chocolate cases to hold chocolate mousse or other fruit mousses
- Serve straight from the freezer as a delicate ice cream

double apricot trifle

Amaretti biscuits are made from apricot kernels, giving you two types of apricot flavour.

To feed more people: Double the ingredients will fill a much larger trifle dish and will make up to 10 portions – you will not need to double the amount of plain chocolate to squirt over.

Serves 4

2 lb (1kg) fresh apricots

1 orange

3 oz (85g) light soft brown sugar

1 tbsp Cointreau

1 tub (250g) mascarpone cheese

1 tub (500ml) ready-made custard

5 oz (150g) amaretti biscuits

1 pack (100g) plain chocolate drops

Oven:

Aga roasting oven, 200C, 400F, Gas 6

Prepare in advance:

Keep in fridge for up to 2 days

Freeze:

Yes

1 Halve the apricots and grate the rind from the orange and squeeze the juice.

2 Set the tub of mascarpone on the back of the Aga to soften and put the unopened pack of chocolate drops onto the back of the Aga to melt.

3 Line the large roasting tin with Bake-O-Glide.

4 Tip the apricots, orange rind and juice into the tin with the sugar and give it a good shake to mix everything together.

5 Hang the tin from the 3rd runners in the roasting oven for about 15 minutes, until the apricots are browned but not quite squashily soft.

6 Remove from the oven and allow to cool.

7 Mix together the mascarpone and custard.

8 Tip the amaretti into a pretty bowl and add the apricots and Cointreau. Pour the custard over and smooth the top.

9 Snip one corner of the bag of chocolate drops and squeeze the melted chocolate in swirls over the top of the trifle.

10 Chill for at least an hour until set, but serve at room temperature.

boxing day trifle

To feed more people: Double the ingredients will fill a vast bowl and feed up to 15. It may be easier to make two trifles the same size, you will still get at least 14 portions.

Serves 6

4 chocolate muffins

3 tbsp kirsch

4 oz caster sugar

6 oz (175g) cranberries

1/4 pint (150ml) orange juice

2 eggs

1 tub (250g) mascarpone

1/4 pint (150ml) thick yogurt

1/2 pint double cream

4 oz (110g) white chocolate

2 oz (55g) plain chocolate

Prepare ahead:

24 hours

Freeze:

No

1 Set the white and plain chocolates in separate bowls on the back of the Aga to melt. Set the mascarpone tub on the back of the Aga to soften.

2 Put the cranberries into a pan with 2 oz (55g) sugar and the orange juice. Heat on the simmering plate and boil gently for 3–5 minutes until soft. Leave to cool.

3 Remove the paper cases from the muffins and slice. Lay the slices in a bowl, and pour over the kirsch. Pour $3/4$ of the cranberries onto the soaked cake.

4 Beat the eggs with the remaining 2 oz (55g) of sugar until pale and fluffy and then beat in the mascarpone and thick yogurt. (Alternatively, use a tub of fresh supermarket custard and beat in the mascarpone and yogurt.) Pile into the bowl on top of the cranberries.

5 Whip the cream, then stir in the white chocolate. Spoon onto the mascarpone, smooth the top and chill until needed. Just before serving, pour over the dark chocolate in swirls and decorate with the remaining cranberries.

cardamom jelly

To serve more people: Double the jelly ingredients (but the same quantity of fruit) will fill a larger mould and will feed 12, especially if there is another pudding offered.

Serves 6

4 tsp powdered gelatine

5 cardamom pods

1/2 pint (300ml) milk

1/4 pint (150ml) double cream

8 oz (225g) caster sugar

3/4 pint (425ml) natural yogurt

To serve:

1 mango

1 lime

Prepare in advance:

Keep in the fridge for 24 hours

Freeze:

No

1 Put the milk, cream and sugar into a pan and gently heat on the simmering plate.

2 Crush the cardamom pods and remove the seeds. Crush the seeds in a pestle and mortar and add to the milk pan. Remove the pan from the heat before it boils.

3 Take 4 tbsp milk from the pan and put into a bowl. Scatter the gelatine over this milk and stir to dissolve. Pour this back into the pan and stir well. Allow to cool.

4 Stir the yogurt into the cooled milk and pour into a ring mould. Chill until set.

5 Dip the mould in hot water and turn out the jelly.

6 Peel and chop the mango and mix with lime juice. Pile the mango into the centre of the jelly and serve.

coffee and walnut tart

To feed more people: Make two tarts for up to 15 people, particularly if there is another pudding on offer. Double the mixture will fill a 12" flan dish and will give up to 15 portions.

Serves 6

Pastry:

6 oz (175g) plain flour

3 oz (75g) butter

1 tbsp caster sugar

1 egg yolk

2 tbsp cold strong black coffee

Filling:

6 oz (175g) walnut halves

3 eggs

3 oz (75g) soft brown sugar

1 tub (200g) mascarpone

3 tbsp strong black coffee

Oven:

Aga roasting oven, 200C, 400F, Gas 6

Prepare in advance:

Cook, cool and refrigerate for up to 24 hours

Prepare ahead:

Keep warm beside the Aga for an hour

Freeze:

Yes

1 To make the pastry, put the flour, sugar, butter, egg yolk into a processor and whizz to the consistency of breadcrumbs. With the motor running, add the coffee a little at a time, until it forms a dough. Roll out and line a 9" (23cm) or 10" (25cm) ceramic flan dish. Refrigerate until needed.

2 Set the mascarpone and coffee in a bowl on the back of the Aga to melt.

3 To assemble the tart, tip the walnuts into the pastry case. Mix together the mascarpone, coffee, sugar and eggs, then pour over the walnuts and set on the floor of the roasting oven.

4 Bake for about 25 minutes, until the pastry is brown and the top risen a little and golden.

5 Dust with icing sugar and serve tepid with crème fraîche.

mango and passion fruit jelly

To feed more people: Double the ingredients will make a huge jelly to give up to 15 portions, or to fill 16 ramekins

Serves 6, more with another pudding

1 litre carton mango and passion fruit juice

5 tsp (2 sachets) gelatine

2 passion fruit

1 Pour a little of the juice into a jam jar and sprinkle on the gelatine. Leave to stand for 5 minutes. Set the jar into a pan of water and bring to the boil in the simmering plate. Stir the mixture in the jar occasionally.

2 Once the gelatine has melted completely, pour it into the rest of the juice and mix well. Pour into a prepared mould or glass bowl and chill until set, about 2–3 hours.

3 Just before serving, halve the passion fruit and scoop out the pips, which you then scatter over the jelly.

chewy meringues

To feed more people: Double the quantity will give at least 15 double meringues, depending upon how large you make them.

Makes up to 8 double meringues

4 egg whites

8 oz (225g) dark brown sugar

Oven:

Aga simmering oven

Prepare in advance:

Will keep in an airtight tin for a week

Prepare ahead:

Do not fill the meringues with cream more than an hour before eating, as they will go soggy while they wait.

Freeze:

Yes

1   Whisk the egg whites until stiff, then add the sugar a spoonful at a time, whisking all the time.

2   Spoon blobs of meringue onto a baking tray lined with Bake-O-Glide (or pipe neatly if you are feeling really keen!) then bake.

3   *4 oven Aga*: Bake the meringues in the warming oven for up to 48 hours.

4   *2 and 3 oven Aga*: Bake in the simmering oven for $1^1/_2$ hours. Transfer the tray to rest between the two Aga lids and allow to continue drying out overnight.

5   Peel off the Bake-O-Glide and allow to cool.

6   Serve with cream and strawberries.

val's new year tiramisu

To feed more people: Double the ingredients will make two large tiramisus, sufficient for 20 with another pudding. You will not need to double the quantity of red wine!

Serves 8

8 oz (225g) ready to eat dried apricots

3 tbsp brandy

3/4 pint (425ml) red wine

6 cloves

1 stick cinnamon

2 tbsp caster sugar

8 oz (225g) pack sponge fingers

1/2 pint (284ml pot) double cream

2 tbsp caster sugar

2 x 7oz (200g) tubs mascarpone

1 pint (500g) tub ready-made custard

Oven:

Back of Aga

Prepare in advance:

Will keep in fridge for up to 48 hours

Freeze:

No

1   Halve the apricots and put into a bowl with the brandy to soak.

2   Set the mascarpone on the back of the Aga to soften.

3   Put the wine, spices and 2 tbsp sugar into a pan and heat gently on the simmering plate until the sugar has dissolved. Set aside to cool.

4   Whip the cream, then fold in 2 tbsp caster sugar, the mascarpone and the custard.

5   Dip the sponge fingers into the mulled wine and arrange half of them on the base of a bowl. Spread half of the apricots on top of the sponge fingers, then pour over half of the cream mixture.

6   Repeat the layers of sponge finger, apricots and custard, then cover and chill for an hour until set.

7   Drink the remaining mulled wine.

8   Sprinkle with ground cinnamon and serve.

water biscuits for cheese

There's not much that says you have made an effort more than home made cheese biscuits!

Serves 4

8 oz (225g) plain flour

$^1/_2$ tsp baking powder

2 oz (55g) butter

1 tbsp Maldon salt

Up to 4 tbsp cold water

Oven:

Baking oven, 180C, 350F, Gas 4

Prepare in advance:

Biscuits will keep in an airtight tin for a week or so

Freeze:

Yes

1 Put the flour, butter, baking powder and half of the salt into a processor and whizz until it resembles breadcrumbs.

2 Add the water, a little at a time, until the mixture comes together as a dough.

3 Roll out the pastry on a floured board and brush with a little water, then scatter over the rest of the salt. Cut into 2"/5cm squares.

4 Lift the biscuits onto the cold plain shelf, lined with Bake-O-Glide, and bake.

5 *3 and 4 oven Aga*: Slide the shelf onto the 3rd runners in the baking oven.

6 *2 oven Aga*: Slide the shelf onto the 4th runners in the roasting oven, with the large roasting tin on the 1st runners above.

7 Bake for about 12 minutes until pale gold. Remove from the oven and transfer to a cooling tray.

8 The biscuits will firm up as they cool.

Alternatives:

• Try using half plain and half wholemeal flour

• Try adding some herbs, dried or fresh, for green biscuits

• Try adding poppy seeds or sesame seeds for speckled biscuits

• Try adding a tablespoonful of grated parmesan cheese to the biscuits

churros

Spanish breakfast fritters, delicious with sticky toffee sauce …

To feed more people: Double the ingredients will make up to 36 churros.

Makes 12–16

4 oz (110g) butter

$^1/_2$ pint (300ml) water

5 oz (150g) plain flour

3 eggs

1$^1/_2$ pints (750ml) vegetable oil for frying

Caster sugar and ground cinnamon to finish

Oven:

Boiling plate

Prepare in advance:

Make the paste and refrigerate for up to 24 hours before cooking

Prepare ahead:

Fried churros will keep warm – on kitchen paper – in the simmering oven for half an hour, but they will not remain crisp

Freeze:

Uncooked mixture only, the fried churros will go soggy as they defrost

1   Put the water and butter into a pan on the simmering plate and heat together until the butter melts.

2   When melted, move to the boiling plate and bring to a fast boil. Tip all of the flour into the pan and beat hard until it is a smooth paste.

3   Allow to cool for about 5 minutes, then beat in the eggs, one at a time. (This is remarkably similar to choux pastry at this stage!)

4   Heat the oil in a deep pan – I tend to put it onto the floor of the roasting oven to heat up, but you may prefer to heat it on the simmering plate where you can keep an eye on it. When it has heated, transfer to the boiling plate to heat further, until it is hot enough to fry and crispen a cube of bread in about 20 seconds – this is about 190C.

5   While the oil is heating, take a piping bag with a $^3/_4$"/1.5cm star nozzle and pipe the paste into 4" lengths. *Or just take spoonsful of the mixture. There should be enough for 12 to 16 blobs.*

6   Drop the paste portions into the oil and fry for 3–4 minutes, turning occasionally, until golden and puffed up. Remove from the oil onto a piece of kitchen paper to drain, sprinkle with caster sugar and ground cinnamon, then serve hot with sticky toffee sauce or a sharp fruit dip or conserve.

sticky apricot cake

To feed more people: Double the ingredients will fill the 11"/28cms sauté pan and will give up to 10 portions – although you will need a very big plate to serve it from!

Serves 4

6 ripe apricots

3 oz (85g) soft brown sugar

8 oz (225g) butter

6 oz (175g) soft brown sugar

2 eggs

3 fl oz (85ml) milk

9 oz (275g) wholemeal self raising flour

4 oz (110g) ground almonds

Oven:

Baking oven, 180C, 375F, Gas 4

Prepare in advance:

Cake will keep in an airtight tin for a couple of days

Freeze:

Yes

1　Cut the apricots in half and remove the stones. Set the butter in a bowl beside the Aga to soften.

2　Tip the sugar into a 10"/25cms heatproof casserole. Set the pan on the boiling plate and swirl 3oz sugar around until it caramelises.

3　Arrange the halved apricots in the caramel, taking care as it is very hot! Set aside.

4　Mix together all the remaining ingredients – if the butter is very soft, this is very quick – then pour the cake mix over the apricots in the pan and bake.

5　*3 and 4 oven Aga*: Put the pan onto the grid shelf on the floor of the baking oven and bake for about 40 minutes until golden.

6　*2 oven Aga*: put the pan into the large roasting tin and hang the tin from the lowest runners in the roasting oven. Slide the cold plain shelf onto the 2nd runners above. Bake for about 25 minutes until the cake has risen and browned, then transfer the whole roasting tin to the simmering oven for a further 20 minutes or so until it has set.

7　Take the cake out of the oven and leave it to stand for about 10 minutes before inverting the pan onto a plate to turn out the cake. Serve at room temperature or tepid, with crème fraîche or yogurt.

haslemere food festival chocolate cake

To feed more people: Double the mixture will fill two 9" tins (bake for an additional 15 minutes) and serve at least 12 to 15. Four times the mixture will fill two 12" tins, needing to bake for twice as long and makes a cake big enough for 30 plus!

Serves 6

6^1/$_2$ oz (185g) self raising flour

1 tbsp golden syrup

2 tbsp cocoa powder

5 oz (150g) caster sugar

2 eggs

1 tsp baking powder

^{1}/$_4$ pint (150ml) milk

^{1}/$_4$ pint (150ml) sunflower oil

Icing:

5 oz (150g) icing sugar

2 oz (55g) butter

1 tbsp milk

2 tbsp cocoa powder

Oven:

Baking oven 180C, 350F, Gas 4

Prepare in advance:

Prepare ahead: Keeps 3 days in a tin, apparently!

Freeze:

Yes

1 Grease and line two 7"/18cm round cake tins.

2 Put all the cake ingredients into a bowl and mix thoroughly.

3 Pour into the prepared tins and bake.

4 *3 and 4 oven Aga*: Put the grid shelf on the 4th runners in the baking oven and set the tins onto the shelf. Bake for about 25 minutes, until risen and springy to touch.

5 *2 oven Aga*: Set the cake tins into the large roasting tin and hang it from the 4th runners in the roasting oven, with the cold shelf on the 2nd runners. Bake for about 20–25 minutes until risen and springy.

6 Remove cakes from the oven and turn out onto wire racks to cool.

7 To make the icing, melt the butter with the cocoa, stir in the milk and sift in the icing sugar. Beat until smooth then use half the mixture to sandwich the cakes together and spread the rest over the top.

apricot and pecan flapjacks

Makes about 16

4 oz (110g) butter

4 oz (110g) demerara sugar

2 tbsp runny honey

6 oz (175g) porridge oats

2 oz (55g) dried apricots

2 oz (55g) pecan nuts

Oven:

Baking oven, 180C, 350F, Gas 4

Prepare ahead:

Flapjacks will keep in an airtight tin for up to 3 days, if no one finds them first

Freeze:

Yes

1 Put the butter, sugar and honey into a pan and set on the simmering plate to melt together.

2 Chop the apricots and nuts.

3 When the butter mixture has melted, stir in the oats, apricots and nuts.

4 Line an 8" square cake tin with Bake-O-Glide and tip the flapjack mixture into it. Smooth the top, then bake.

5 *3 and 4 oven Aga*: set the grid shelf on the 4th runners in the baking oven and bake for about 15 minutes until golden.

6 *2 oven Aga*: Put the cake tin into the large roasting tin and hang from the lowest runners in the roasting oven, then slide the cold plain shelf onto the 2nd runners above. Bake for about 15 minutes until golden.

7 Allow the flapjacks to cool in the tin for 5 minutes, then turn out onto a cooling rack.

Alternatives:

• Try using chocolate drops instead of the apricots and nuts

• Try using chopped dates or walnuts instead of the apricots or pecans

kate ransom's passion cake

To feed more people: Double the ingredients will fill a 10" tin and serve up to 20, four times will fill a 12" tin, which will give 50 slices or more

Serves 6–8

6 fl oz (180ml) corn oil

6 oz (175g) caster sugar

3 eggs

1 tsp vanilla extract

8 oz (225g) carrots

4 oz (110g) walnuts

6 oz (175g) plain flour

1 tsp bicarbonate of soda

1 tsp baking powder

1 tsp cinnamon

1 tsp salt

Topping:

3 oz (85g) cream cheese

2 oz (55g) butter

1/2 tsp vanilla extract

4 oz (110g) icing sugar

12 walnut halves to decorate

Oven:

Baking oven, 160C, 350F, Gas 4

Prepare in advance:

Without the topping, the cooked cake will keep in a tin for up to a week. (Hide the tin!)

Freeze:

Yes, with or without the topping

1 Grate the carrots and chop the walnuts.

2 Mix all the cake ingredients together and pour into an 8"/20cms square cake tin, lined with Bake-O-Glide.

3 *3 and 4 oven Aga:* Set the grid shelf on the floor of the baking oven and put the cake tin onto it. Bake for an hour, maybe an hour and a quarter, until firm and golden.

4 *2 oven Aga:* Set the cake tin into the large roasting tin and slide into the roasting tin on the lowest runners. Slide the plain shelf onto the 2nd runners above. Bake for about half an hour until the top is set and browned, then transfer the entire roasting tin to the 3rd runners in the simmering oven for at least an hour, until the cake is firm. Don't forget to take the plain shelf out of the roasting oven to cool down!

5 When the cake has cooked, remove from the oven and cool in the tin.

6 For the topping: Mix the cream cheese, icing sugar and butter with the vanilla. Spread over the top and sides of the cake and decorate with walnut halves.

chocolate and orange nut bars

To feed more people: Double the quantity will fill the large roasting tin and make 48 squares

Serves 6

Base:

6 oz (175) plain flour

3 oz (75g) caster sugar

3 oz (75g) butter

2 drops vanilla extract

1 egg yolk

1/4 tsp salt

Topping:

1 pack (100g) pecan nuts

1 pack (100g) plain chocolate drops

Grated rind of an orange

Juice of half an orange

3 oz (75g) butter

3 oz (75g) caster sugar

1 oz (25g) plain flour

1 egg

1 egg white

Oven:

Baking oven, 180C, 350F, Gas 4

Prepare in advance:

Bars will keep in a tin for up to 3 days if carefully hidden!

Freeze:

Yes

1   For the base, whizz all ingredients together in a processor.

2   Line the small roasting tin with Bake-O-Glide and tip in the base. Press down firmly.

3   Pile the topping ingredients into the processor bowl and whizz together. Pour the topping over the base and smooth the top.

4   *3 and 4 oven Aga*: Hang the tin on the 3rd set of runners in the baking oven for 20–30 minutes until golden.

5   *2 oven Aga*: Set the tin into the large roasting tin and hang it from the lowest runners in the roasting oven, with the cold shelf on the 2nd runners. Cook for about 20–30 minutes until golden.

6   Allow to cool in the tin, then turn onto a cooling rack and cut into 24 bars. Serve warm as a pudding with some natural yogurt, or cold for tea.

fruity coffee cake

To feed more people: Double the mixture will fill a 10" cake tin and should give 12 plus portions. Bake for 15 minutes longer.

Serves 6

5 oz (150g) self raising flour

6 oz (175g) wholemeal self raising flour

1/2 tsp baking powder

4 oz (110g) butter

3 oz (75g) soft brown sugar

3 eggs

4 oz (110g) black treacle

6 oz (175g) sultanas

2 oz (55g) stem ginger

1 cup espresso coffee

Small tub (250ml) crème fraîche

Oven:

Baking oven, 180C, 350F, Gas 4

Prepare in advance:

Cake will keep in a tin for up to 3 days

Freeze:

Yes

1   Grate the ginger. Line an 8"/20cms square cake tin with Bake-O-Glide.

2   Measure the black treacle into a pan. Add the butter, sultanas, ginger and sugar. Set onto the simmering plate to melt.

3   Mix together the flours and baking powder.

4   Once the treacle mixture has melted, tip it onto the flour, add the eggs and beat together. Pour into the prepared tin.

5   *3 and 4 oven Aga*: Set the tin on the grid shelf on the floor of the baking oven bake for about an hour.

6   *2 oven Aga*: Set the tin into the large roasting tin and hang it from the lowest runners in the roasting oven, with the cold shelf on the 2nd runners. Cook for about half an hour, then transfer the roasting tin and its contents to the simmering oven for about 45–50 minutes. Take the plain shelf from the oven and allow to cool before putting back into the cupboard!

7   Bake until the centre of the cake is firm.

8   Take the cake from the oven and allow to cool for a few minutes, then tip over the hot, strong coffee.

9   Serve warm, with the crème fraîche.

cheats barm brack

For a large tea party, two loaves will be plenty for 12 people as long as there are other cakes.

Serves 4

1 pack (500g) white bread mix

2 oz (55g) butter

2 oz (55g) caster sugar

1 egg

About 1/2 pint (300ml) milk

12 oz (350g) sultanas

1 lemon

Topping:

1 oz (25g) butter

1 tsp ground cinnamon

1/2 tsp ground mixed spice

Oven:

Roasting oven, 200C, 400F, Gas 6

Prepare in advance:

Dough will rise slowly in fridge overnight

Prepare ahead:

Keeps in an airtight tin for 24 hours if you hide the tin!

Freeze:

Yes

1 Put the milk in a mug on the back of the Aga to warm up a little.

2 Squeeze the juice from the lemon and add to the sultanas, with a tablespoon of warm water. Set on the back of the Aga to plump up.

3 Tip the bread mix, sugar and butter into a processor and whizz until mixed, or rub the butter in by hand. Mix together the egg and about half of the warmed milk, and add to the flour mixture. Mix with a round bladed knife and add the rest of the milk slowly until it is a soft dough – you may not need all of the milk.

4 Knead the dough by hand or in a processor until it is really pliable.

5 Drain the sultanas and knead them into the dough.

6 Line an 8" cake tin with Bake-O-Glide and put the dough into it. Set beside the Aga for about an hour, until it has doubled in size.

7 Put the butter and spices for the topping in a bowl on the back of the Aga to melt.

8 Bake the tin on the floor of the roasting oven for about 30 minutes until golden brown.

9 As soon as the loaf comes out of the oven, pour the flavoured, melted butter over it.

crunchy chocolate cake

To feed more people: Double the mixture will fill a 10" deep tin. You will get up to 20 portions from this. Four times the mixture will fill a 12" tin and you will get about 40 portions. Bake for an extra 20 minutes.

Serves 6–8

8 oz (225g) butter

6 oz (175g) soft brown sugar

8 oz (225g) plain chocolate

3 oz (75g) plain flour

4 oz (110g) ground almonds

6 eggs

1/4 tsp vanilla extract

2 oz (55g) caster sugar

Oven:

Baking oven, 170C, 325F, Gas 3

Prepare in advance:

Cake will keep in a tin for up to 3 days

Freeze:

Yes

1 Set the butter beside the Aga to soften.

2 Break up the chocolate and set it in a bowl on the Aga to melt for about 20 minutes.

3 Separate the eggs.

4 Line an 8"/20cms square cake tin with Bake-O-Glide.

5 Beat the butter with the chocolate, brown sugar, egg yolks, flour, almonds and vanilla.

6 Whisk the egg whites and fold into the mixture. Pour into the prepared tin and scatter with the caster sugar.

7 *3 and 4 oven Aga*: Set the tin on the grid shelf on the floor of the baking oven bake for about an hour and a half – you may need to slide the cold shelf onto the 2nd runners after about 50 minutes.

8 *2 oven Aga*: Set the tin into the large roasting tin and hang it from the lowest runners in the roasting oven, with the cold shelf on the 2nd runners. Cook for about half an hour, then transfer the roasting tin and its contents to the simmering oven for about an hour.

9 Bake until the centre of the cake is firm.

10 Take the cake from the oven and allow to cool for a few minutes, before turning out onto a wire rack.

spiced apple cake

To feed more people: Double the ingredients will fill a 10" / 25cms tin and four times the ingredients will fill a 12" / 30cms tin, or the large roasting tin and should give at least 30 portions

Serves 6–8

6 oz (150g) butter

6 oz (175g) soft brown sugar

3 eggs

8 oz (225g) self raising flour

$1/2$ tsp ground allspice

$1/2$ tsp ground cinnamon

$1/2$ tsp grated nutmeg

2 large Bramley apples

2 tbsp demerara sugar

Icing sugar to finish

Oven:

Baking oven, 180C, 350F, Gas 4

Prepare in advance:

Cake will keep in airtight tin for a day or so

Prepare ahead:

Keep warm beside the Aga for an hour or two before serving

Freeze:

Yes

1 Set the butter in a bowl beside the Aga to soften for half an hour or so.

2 Line an 8"/20cms square deep cake tin with Bake-O-Glide.

3 Peel, core and slice the apples.

4 Put the sugar, butter, eggs, flour and spices into a bowl and mix thoroughly.

5 Tip half of the cake mixture into the prepared tin, then add the sliced apples. Spread the rest of the cake mixture over the apples. Scatter the demerara sugar over the mix in the tin.

6 *3 and 4 oven Aga*: Set the grid shelf on the floor of the oven and put the cake tin onto it. Bake for about an hour, until the cake is golden and set

7 *2 oven Aga*: Set the cake tin into the large roasting tin and hang it from the 4th runners in the roasting oven. Slide the cold plain shelf onto the 2nd runners. Bake for about half an hour, until the top has risen and set and is quite brown enough, then transfer the entire roasting tin to the simmering oven for a further hour. Don't forget to take the plain shelf out of the oven to cool down!

8 Allow the cake to cool in the tin until tepid, sprinkle with icing sugar and serve with cream or custard. Or both!

party menu planning

Putting together a menu for a party can be more stressful than cooking it, or it can be as much fun as the cooking.

There are a few guidelines to follow when planning a menu which make it easy:

- **You need a good balance of colours** – there's not a lot of colour in a dinner that has a mushroom soup to start, a beef casserole and a chocolate pudding, even though it would be delicious!

- **You need a good balance of textures** – a savoury mousse for a starter and a lemon mousse for pudding leave no crunch, whereas a mushroom tart for a starter, followed by a quiche, with a pie for pudding will be too filling for many and lacks imagination.

- **You need a good balance of flavours** – a fish starter followed by a fish main course might be too much for some.

- **You probably need less food than you think** – particularly if people are helping themselves, they tend to take less than if you dole out the food onto plates and hand them out!

- **If you have a themed meal, stick to the theme throughout** – a wonderful selection of curries for a main course needs either no starter at all, or something in keeping like onion bhajis and a selection of dips with naan bread, then either no pudding other than fruit, or one that keeps the theme going.

- **Get ahead** – if you are entertaining on a night when you will possibly arrive home late, prepare as much as you can in advance. It is far less stressful to have most of the meal assembled and in the fridge so that you can come in, shove it all into the Aga then go and change to welcome your guests, rather than greeting them frazzled with nothing cooked. Even if you are at home all afternoon, the more you have done ahead, the more relaxed a host you will be and the more you will enjoy your party.

- **Relax** – your guests have come to enjoy your company and lovely food is a bonus. It is possible to try too hard with a very elaborate meal and then you miss out on most of the party if you are in the kitchen!

menu suggestions

1. Curry nights!

Double the starter and pudding and one recipe quantity of each main course dish will feed up to 15 people.

Most of this can be prepared in advance and refrigerated, to reheat before eating.

Onion bhajis to start

Lamb rogan josh
Tandoori chicken
Chicken korma
Aga rice
Daal (either plain or aubergine and tomato daal)
Cucumber raita
Naan breads
Poppadoms

Cardamom and yogurt jelly for pudding

2. Thai night in

Small bowls of the soup, one recipe quantity of the main course dishes and one quantity of the pudding will feed 8 people.

Most of this needs last-minute cooking, but you can prepare all the herbs and spices and chop all the ingredients in advance to make the actual cooking very quick.

Hot and sour noodle soup to start

Chiang mai stir fry
Thai beef salad
Thai vegetable curry
Aga rice

Cardamom custard tart for pudding

3. Summer lunch in the garden

Double the ingredients for the starter, one recipe quantity of each of the main course and pudding dishes will feed up to 10 people.

Most of this is served cold (or at room temperature) so you can prepare much of it in advance and refrigerate until an hour or so before serving. Do not dress any salads until just before eating them, the dressing will make the vegetables wilt.

Avocado, prawn and mango salad with fresh bread to start

Summer cod with oranges and tomatoes
Cumin chicken salad
Pepper and aubergine salad
Summer vegetable salad
Oven steamed new potatoes

Double apricot trifle with hazelnut biscuits for pudding, with
Honey and ginger peaches

4. Rained-off summer lunch, not in the garden!

Double the ingredients for the starter, one recipe quantity of each of the main course and pudding dishes will feed up to 10 people.

Most of this can be prepared in advance – make the dip, assemble the tart and kebabs, prepare the vegetables for the salads and make the pastry for the tart and the lemon creams. Refrigerate everything then cook at the last minute.

Aubergine dip with warm pitta bread to start

Asparagus tart
Marinated monkfish kebabs
Chickpea and chorizo salad
Warm pea and potato salad

Gooseberry crumble tart for pudding, with
Lemon and lime creams

5. Smart summer dinner party

Much of this can be prepared in advance: Assemble the tarts and refrigerate, chop all the sea bass ingredients and refrigerate, bake the roulade and chill or freeze. All you need to do on the night is take it all out of the fridge and bake the tarts and fish.

Creamy asparagus tarts

Steamed sea bass
Aga rice
Big green salad

Lemon and honey roulade for pudding, with a bowl of summer fruit

Cheese and home made water biscuits

6. Smart autumn dinner party

Much of this can be prepared in advance: Make the mushrooms pots and refrigerate, cook the duck casserole and refrigerate (skim off any fat once it has set in the fridge), prepare the tart and refrigerate. All you need to do on the night is take it all out of the fridge and shove it into the oven to reheat while you get ready!

Warm mushroom pots to start

Spiced orange duck
Couscous
Steamed broccoli and sugar snaps

Crunchy pear tart for pudding

Cheese and home made water biscuits

7. Smart winter dinner party

Most of this can be prepared in advance: make the fish balls and sauce and refrigerate, poach the pheasant and make the sauce, assemble and refrigerate, make the jelly and refrigerate, assemble the strudel and refrigerate. All you need to do on the night is take it all out of the fridge and put it into the ovens!

Smoked cod balls with pea sauce to start
Pheasant cream
Mashed potatoes
Glazed carrots

Mango and passionfruit jelly for pudding, with
Pear, cranberry and almond strudel

Cheese and home made water biscuits

8. Smart spring dinner party

Most of this can be prepared in advance, cook the soufflés and sauce and freeze or refrigerate, brown the beef and make the Wellington and freeze or refrigerate, then all you have to do on the night is reheat the starter, bake the main course and throw the pudding together!

Twice-baked goats' cheese soufflés in tomato sauce, to start

Beef Wellington
Foolproof sliced potatoes
Green vegetable

Upside down toffee pudding
Cheese and home made water biscuits

9. Easter family lunch

Spinach and blue cheese tart, to start

Italian lamb casserole
Mashed root vegetables
Green vegetable

Raspberry brioche pudding

10. Spring bank holiday family supper

*Most of this can be prepared in advance, all you need to do
on the night is cook the chicken*

Mushroom salad gougère, to start

Springtime chicken

Chocolate goo pudding

11. Bonfire night supper

Swede and sweet potato soup with crusty bread, served in mugs around the bonfire
Cheese and bacon potato pancakes, served in paper napkins around the bonfire

Tamarind chicken
Aga rice
Lentil and vegetable bake
Green vegetable, all served indoors to warm up after the fireworks

Raspberry frangipane tart for pudding

12. Half term family invasion supper

Prawn and rocket risotto to start

Smart sausages
Foolproof sliced potatoes
Chunky roasted squash

Passion fruit cheesecake for pudding

13. Boxing Day lunch – anything but turkey will do today!

*Roast the potatoes in advance and freeze – defrost in the roasting oven for 20 minutes,
make the tiramisu in advance and refrigerate until needed*

Horseradish crusted roast beef
Roast potatoes
Roasted sesame sprouts

New year tiramisu for pudding, with green fruit salad for anyone who has had enough
calories over Christmas!

index